THE ORIGIN OF MAGIC
AND RELIGION

GREAT MOTHER TYPES

(1) Shell type (Thrace)
(2) Shell type (Susa)
(3) Mother-pot type (Hissarlik)
(4) Human type (Aurignacian)

THE ORIGIN OF MAGIC AND RELIGION

BY

W. J. PERRY, M.A.

KENNIKAT PRESS
Port Washington, N. Y./London

THE ORIGIN OF MAGIC AND RELIGION

First published in 1923
Reissued in 1971 by Kennikat Press
Library of Congress Catalog Card No: 73-118543
ISBN 0-8046-1168-8

Manufactured by Taylor Publishing Company   Dallas, Texas

PREFACE

IN this small book I have tried to tell, as clearly as possible, the story of the development of magical and religious thought and practice. For some years work has been proceeding in this country on the historical aspect of the growth of civilization. As the result of this work, the general principles of development of various forms of human culture have become fairly clear, and it seems time to give the general reader some account of the progress made up to the present.

As is usual in the case of a new branch of study, it seems certain now that much of the work of early workers on the origins of religion and magic will have to be undone. They have accomplished work of incalculable value in collecting great masses of facts, and in discovering what are the problems to be solved. It is the privilege of the present and of the coming generations to stand on the shoulders of those who have gone before, and to attempt the solution of the problems that have been formulated. It is not given to any man, or any group of men, to see the whole of the light. Thought is always conditioned by circumstances. If the present volume does record certain advances in the study of magic and religion, it is certain that, in time, we shall see clearly many things that are now dark. At the same time I fervently hope that, by the adoption of a strictly historical attitude towards humanistic studies, a solid footing will have been gained, so that future generations will be able to proceed on their way with confidence.

I have confined myself, in this volume, to religion and magic. At the same time, it has been necessary to explain briefly certain secular matters, such as those concerning the manner of spread of early culture. In the companion volume, on *The Growth of Civilization*, I propose to discuss these matters in greater detail.

Although this book is intended primarily for the general reader, it is commended to the specialist, partly because it attempts to tell the story of religious development, and partly because it embodies the results of original research. The most important new topic treated here is that of immortality. I have urged that it was this belief, formulated by the Egyptians in early dynastic times, that constituted one of the most powerful incentives to action that man has ever possessed, an incentive which led to a world-wide spread of culture as the result of the search for the Earthly Paradise. I have urged, moreover, that the belief, so widespread throughout the world in all ages, that a ritual death and rebirth was the necessary prelude to immortality, was the direct outcome of the Egyptian practice of mummification, in connection with which practice the idea of immortality arose. In an Appendix I have argued that the change of name which occurs in connection with ritual death and rebirth, is also an outcome of the practice of mummification.

It is a great pleasure to thank several kind friends for their help and advice. Professor Canney and Mr. F. W. Halliday of Manchester University, the Rev. H. Lawton, and Mr. W. Grindrod of the Secondary School, Chorley, as well as members of my classes in Comparative Religion in the University, have helped me, by their criticisms and suggestions, to express myself more clearly, and to them I express my thanks. Miss Dorothy Davison has drawn for me some of the types of the Great Mother images, and I wish to express here my indebtedness to her. I am much obliged to my sister, Miss D. C. Perry, for making the index.

W. J. PERRY

MANCHESTER,
June, 1923

CONTENTS

THE ORIGIN OF MAGIC AND RELIGION

CHAPTER I

THE BEGINNINGS

THE study of magic and religion has a ready appeal to the sympathies of every thinking man and woman. For the beliefs and practices of mankind during the ages afford a revelation of their innermost thoughts and longings. By means of this study we come to understand how our remote ancestors faced the eternal questions of life and death, and in what way they solved these problems. We can understand how, as civilization grew and developed, men's thoughts were moulded into fresh forms, and their attention turned to fresh objects of contemplation.

The aim of this book is to trace, so far as is in my power, the main lines of development of thought that have led to the production of the different religious and magical systems that exist among men. My endeavour will be to show that the process must be viewed as one of growth from very simple beginnings. Man has had to make his discoveries in the realm of magic and religion, as in other depart-

ments of knowledge : his magical and religious
beliefs and practices have not sprung spontaneously from his brain, in direct response
to some innate mental capacities. On the
contrary, each of these magical and religious
beliefs and practices has a history that must
be studied, and each stage in its growth has
to be explained. None can be taken for
granted, or explained away by some facile
extemporization. In order to understand how
this process of growth has taken place, it is
necessary to put on one side all *a priori* speculative notions as to the manner of development
of human society, and to pursue a pure historical
inquiry, beginning at the earliest possible
date, and following the threads down through
the ages as well as is possible, picking them
up, when broken, at the next possible place,
relying on nothing but what is patent fact,
or what can directly be inferred therefrom.
The study of human society has been vitiated
in the past by the application of unrestrained
speculation to matters that were often capable
of easy verification ; and this uncritical habit
has worked infinite damage to thought, leading
to the practice of inventing explanations of
facts, instead of inquiring strictly into the
real meaning of these facts. This practice
will have to be repressed, if any progress is
to be made. And no better method of repression
can be adopted than the application of the
historical method of inquiry. Once events are
ranged in their historical sequence, the facts

soon begin to tell their own story, and speculation can be laid on one side as unnecessary.

I shall therefore begin at a point where,
beyond doubt, we stand at the beginning of
human history, at that point in time when
men of our own species, not ape-like men, but
men with modern brains, first appeared on
the scene in western Europe, in what is termed
the Aurignacian stage of culture, and took up
their dwellings in the caves and rock-shelters
of France, Spain and other countries, thus
ringing up the curtain on the first act of the
drama of civilization. Where they came from
we do not know; but on their arrival they
had already made some advance in the arts
and crafts : they made implements, usually
of flint or chert, for domestic and hunting
purposes ; they painted, on the walls and
ceilings of the caves where they lived, pictures
of animals, such as the bear, bison, mammoth,
and so forth ; they were sculptors, and have
left behind them many examples of their art ;
their burial customs also bear witness to the
possession of a certain degree of culture (1).

The study of the art and of the funerary
customs of these early men shows clearly
that they had made some considerable progress
in thought, that they had reasoned about
their relations to the outside world, and had
devised means to enable them to procure
food, to gain protection from danger, and to
ameliorate the lot of the dead.

The paintings are invariably found in the

deep recesses of the caves, in dark hidden galleries, often difficult of access. They depict two classes of animals, those hunted for food, and dangerous beasts of prey. It seems certain that, in both cases, the aim of the paintings was to enable men to gain control over these animals, to cause the animals that were eaten to be captured the more easily, and, in the case of the dangerous beasts, to gain some measure of protection from them. The desire to gain protection will be made more apparent shortly when the funerary rites are considered. The use of paintings to get food is the first known instance of the preoccupation of man with his food supply; and it will be found that, as thought developed, man was always thinking earnestly about the same thing. Rites connected with the fertility of cattle, and with the procuring of crops, have always formed part of the religious systems of man, and, indeed, in some instances they have constituted the most prominent part of the religious and magical ritual.

Man does not live by bread alone, nor does he confine his activities, even when so lowly in culture as when he was in the Aurignacian phase of the Stone Age, to devising means for getting food. He thought of other things, of life and death, of health and disease, and his thoughts expressed themselves in actions. Early men in the cave period buried their dead, usually in a crouching position, often packed round with red earth, the body being provided with necklaces of teeth, usually of wild animals that were hunted, bits of stone and bone, and shells. These objects were evidently placed in the grave with deliberate intent : for, to take one instance, in a cave at Laugerie Basse, in France, certain cowrie shells from the Indian Ocean were distributed about the body, two on the forehead, one by each arm, and four at the knees, a form of arrangement that obviously was purposive (2).

It is now becoming possible, on the basis of wide surveys of the evidence derived from human societies in all times and all places, to give an interpretation of these customs of the Stone Age. Let us take in turn the red coloured earth that was placed round the body in the grave, the shells and the animal's teeth, and see what they probably meant to early man. Obviously our remote ancestors have not left any direct record of their intent, but it is possible to guess fairly certainly at their aims. The world owes to Professor Elliot Smith the explanation of these early burial practices (3). He has pointed out that some of the cave paintings depict animals with arrows implanted in their flanks near the region of the heart ; sometimes the heart itself is shown, which is evidence that these men recognized the importance of that organ for the life of the animal. These facts suggest that early man knew that death was the result of physical injury. Since death by physical injury is usually accompanied by the loss of blood, Elliot Smith argues that death was, for our remote ancestors, nothing more than lack of blood. That being so, these men evidently thought that, by giving back blood to the dead, they could be reanimated. For, according to Elliot Smith, the red colouring matter that accompanied the dead was regarded as a substitute for blood. The burial practices of the Chinese show that this interpretation is probably correct : they bury their dead in coffins made of woods that are supposed to have the power of giving life to the dead ; and they adorn the corpse with all manner of substances for the same purpose. Death, for them, as probably for primitive man in Europe, was but a sleep and a forgetting.

Elliot Smith has also explained the meaning of the shells that were used by early men in Europe :—" If the loss of blood was at first the only recognized cause of death, the act of birth was clearly the only process of lifegiving. The portal by which a child entered the world was regarded, therefore, not only as the channel of birth, but also as the actual giver of life. The large Red Sea cowrie shell, which closely simulates this ' giver of life,' then came to be endowed by popular imagination with the same powers. Hence the shell was used in the same way as red ochre or carnelian : it was placed in the grave to confer vitality on the dead, and worn on bracelets and necklaces to secure good luck by using the ' giver of life ' to avert the risk of danger to life" (4).

Elliot Smith then goes on to explain how the uses of the cowrie shell as a " giver of life " came to be extended. " At first it was probably its more general powers of averting death or giving vitality to the dead that played the more obtrusive part in the magical use of the shell. But the circumstances which led to the development of the shell's symbolism naturally and inevitably conferred upon the cowrie shell special power over women. It was the surrogate of the life-giving organ. It became an amulet to increase the fertility of women and to help them in child-birth. It was, therefore, worn by girls suspended from a girdle, so as to be as near as possible to the organ it was supposed to simulate and whose potency it was supposed· to be able to reinforce and intensify. Just as bracelets and necklaces of carnelian were used to confer on either sex the vitalizing virtues of blood, which it was supposed to simulate, so also cowries, or imitations of them made of metal or stone, were worn as bracelets, necklaces, or hair ornaments, to confer health and good luck on both sexes " (5).

If red substances seem to be connected with death, and shells with life, so the teeth worn in necklaces seem to be connected with protection. Bears, wild boars, lions, tigers, mammoths are dangerous animals, which protect themselves with their teeth and claws. At the present day many peoples of low culture believe that the wearing of parts of the body of a dangerous animal, particularly a tooth or claw, gives protection from danger ; so it is legitimate to believe that early man thought to bring himself, by means of teeth and claws, under the special protection of the original possessors of these instruments of offence and defence, though it is by no means easy to formulate the exact form of reasoning that led him to invent this custom.

When we consider these activities as a whole, it is evident that objects such as cowrie shells, red ochre, and animals' teeth could be called *Magical*, and their use could be called *Magic*.

By the aid of certain substances or objects, or by means of certain acts, men believe, in certain circumstances, that they can influence each other, and also natural phenomena, for their own advantage. So, when the men of the Upper Palæolithic Age used teeth, shells, and red ochre, they were laying the foundations of magical practice for the ages that followed. Elliot Smith has summarized this activity of man in one of the most important generalizations ever made in the domain of religion and magic. He says :—" In delving into the remotely distant history of our species we cannot fail to be impressed with the persistence with which, throughout the whole of his career, man (of the species *Sapiens*) has been seeking for an elixir of life, to give added ' vitality ' to the dead (whose existence was not consciously regarded as ended), to prolong the days of active life to the living, to restore youth, and to protect his own life from all assaults, not merely of time, but also of circumstances. In other words, the elixir he sought was something that would bring him ' good luck ' in all the events of life and its continuation. Most of the amulets, even of modern times, the lucky trinkets, the averters of the ' Evil Eye,' the practices and devices for securing good luck in love and sport, in curing bodily ills or mental distress, in attaining material prosperity, or a continuance of existence after death, are survivals of this ancient and persistent striving after those objects which our earliest forefathers called collectively ' Givers of Life ' " (6).

The early men of the cave-dwelling age chose their givers of life from the fundamental facts of life and death as they knew them. The loss of blood is the cause of death ; the portal of life is the giver thereof : these are legitimate inferences for ignorant men to make. Likewise, the idea that what protected wild animals could be made to protect men was, in a way, logical. The use of bits of bone probably also is due to the idea that they can give life to the living. But men were not content to satisfy themselves with a few objects. From these simple beginnings a vast ramification issued. Considering the nature of the " drive " that forced him on, it is not surprising to find that early man soon added fresh objects and substances to his battery of life-givers. Red was the colour of blood, so every red substance could be a surrogate of blood : thus carnelian,

hæmatite, red ochre, red coral were used in
early times, and still are used as amulets and
charms, even in this country, on account of
their supposed life-giving qualities : red flowers
and red berries also came to be used to give
life and health and to ward off danger. The
use of shells shows in like manner how men
will apply ideas that came to be connected, for
some reason or other, with one object or substance, to another similar object or substance.
The kind of shell first used by the men of France
for necklaces is not known. In the caves
all sorts have been found, including the peri-
winkle, mussel and snail. Evidently the idea,
attached perhaps in the beginning to one
kind of shell, spread to others. But the most
important of all was the cowrie, which has
had a fascinating history. Its first known
appearance, in the caves of Southern France,
is romantic (7). How came the men living in
remote ages on the south coast of France,
into possession of Indian Ocean shells ? We
do not know. We do know, however, that the
Red Sea, famed for its cowries, was the home
of other shells that played an important part
in early beliefs regarding life-givers. The conch
shell, the spider shell, the pearl-shell, and
others became possessed of life-giving properties,
and in their turn transmitted their powers
to other shells. For instance, all pearl-bearing
shells, such as the mussel, the clam and the
Tridacna, came to be regarded as life-giving,
and to be used for the same purposes as pearls

and the mother-of-pearl shell. In like manner, the Red Sea spider shell, with its arm-like processes, seems to have caused the octopus and other cephalopods in the Mediterranean to have become objects of attention, and to be figured on vases of the early period in the Ægean as personifying the fertilizing powers of water. This is probably because the arm-like processes of the Red Sea spider shell resemble the arms of the octopus, so that men coming from the Red Sea to the Mediterranean would, in the absence of the spider shell, substitute for. it the octopus, argonaut, and other sea-animals (8). Any resemblance, real or fancied, sufficed to cause the inclusion of an object in the armoury of life-givers. In consequence of this, multitudes of substances have been used, at one time or other, as charms, amulets, averters of the Evil Eye, and so on ; but all have come into currency as the result of the working of the same process of transference. On so simple a basis has been built up a vast structure of practice.

Not only did the objects that were first of all identified with the body come to set out on a career of their own, and transfer their powers to other, similar objects, but the original source and fount of these objects, the human body, was destined to provide yet other life-givers. For instance, as knowledge of anatomy increased, the functions of other organs than the portal of life became known. We find, for instance, that the Egyptians had devised

the notion of a Magic Wand, that has been
of such value to magicians throughout the ages.
It has been shown conclusively that this
idea was derived from the functions of the
uterus.   The uterus gives life, and it is associated
with the opening of the portal of life, by which
we all enter the world.   Therefore the magic
wand has these two great powers ; it opens
doors and it gives life.   The male organ of
generation came, in later times, to be regarded
as a giver of life, as did the eye also, so closely
connected with our life, and with the expression
of the personality.   The hand and the leg
have also played their part in the history of
amulets.

It is striking to observe the persistency with
which men have continued to use certain objects
as life-givers.   Once an object comes into
currency, it tends to stay there.   The earliest
known necklaces had on them shells, teeth,
bits of bone and pebbles.   Inquire in later
ages, and you will find the same objects still
used on necklaces, right down to the present
day in Europe.   As one material after another
is incorporated, it remains in position.   Jet
and amber first appear in the so-called neolithic
age, and they still continue in use, though
mainly now for ornament.   As a striking
instance of the persistence with which men
will cling to the use of a particular substance
or colour, the case of red coral may be mentioned.   The pre-dynastic Egyptians used it
for beads, doubtless on account of its colour.

In later times the Greeks made great use of
it, and they communicated the practice, among
so many other things, to the Celts, who evidently
originated their peculiar culture in central
Europe under Greek and Etruscan influence.
After the conquest of India by Alexander the
Great, the Greeks opened up a trade with
India, took red coral there, and sold so much
that the supply in the Mediterranean ran
short, and the Celts consequently could get
none. The Celts were not at a loss : they
promptly borrowed from the Greeks the practice of making red enamel, originally invented
by the Egyptians, and continued, down to the
time of their conversion to Christianity, to
adorn their harness and armour, and to make
their necklaces, of red enamel, in place of red
coral (9).

One important event in the world's history
can be explained as the result of the study of
givers of life—the use of gold. The realization
of this we owe, like so many other things, to
Elliot Smith. I quote his words :—" With
the introduction of the practice of wearing
shells on girdles and necklaces and as hair
ornaments, the time arrived when people living
some distance from the sea experienced difficulty
in obtaining these amulets in quantities sufficient
to meet their demands. Hence they resorted
to the manufacture of imitations of these shells
in clay and stone. But at an early period in
their history the inhabitants of the deserts
between the Nile and the Red Sea discovered

that they could make more durable and attractive models of cowries and other shells by using the plastic yellow metal which was lying about in these deserts unused and unappreciated. This practice first gave to the metal gold an arbitrary value which it did not possess before. For the peculiar live-giving attributes of the shells modelled in the yellow metal came to be transferred to the metal itself. No doubt the lightness and especially the beauty of such gold models appealed to the early Egyptians, and were in large measure responsible for the hold gold acquired over mankind. But this was an outcome of the empirical knowledge gained from a practice that originally was inspired purely by cultural and not æsthetic motives " (10).

The use of gold as currency likewise is derived by Elliot Smith from the use of cowries for that purpose. In many parts of the world cowrie or other shells form the currency, even in countries long away from the natural source of supply of such shells. Elliot Smith suggests that the great demand for cowrie shells for ornaments and amulets caused people to exchange all manner of articles for them, and thus to make them into a currency. So gold, when it was associated with the cowrie, also became a currency.

Another important consequence of the use of objects chosen for their life-giving properties was the adoption of the use of clothing. The wearing of clothes is in no way natural to men ;

several existing tribes still go about stark
naked, except, perhaps, for a few beads, or
some other form of simple ornament, worn for
the life-giving properties of the objects or substances of which they are composed (11). In the
Sudan and elsewhere women wear girdles of
cowrie shells to give them fertility. It probably
was by way of this practice that the use of
clothing arose ; for women would find that
their sexual attractiveness was thereby en-
hanced. Probably, also, the early ruling classes
would begin to use clothes to add to their
dignity.

That the earliest use of clothing was purely
ornamental is beyond doubt. It was in no
way due to a feeling of shame at exposure of
the person, such as would be experienced by
a modern European in a similar situation.
That shame was a consequence of the use of
clothing ; it was not the cause of it. In like
manner jewellery and ornaments generally
originated in givers of life. It can safely be
said that every substance used in this way
was originally a "giver of life," and that it
still is so regarded among peoples less sophisti-
cated than ourselves. The belief in lucky and
unlucky stones, that still persists among us,
shows that these ideas die hard.

THE GREAT MOTHER

The caves of western Europe contain traces
of the beginnings, not only of magic, but also

of *Religion*. The early artists were sculptors
as well as painters ; and, in addition to depict-
ing animals, they carved figures of women,
but not of men. These figurines did not
represent the natural proportions of the female
figure, but, as is shown by Fig. 4 of the Plate,
exaggerated certain parts beyond all reason.
This is remarkable for people who could depict
the figure of a wild boar in a manner to excite
our admiration. They were not crude crafts-
men, but knew what effect they wanted to
get, and how to get it. When they made
these feminine images with the hips, and other
parts of the body, grossly exaggerated, they
were undoubtedly working with deliberate intent.
Their probable purpose has been suggested
by Elliot Smith. The cowrie shell, as the
symbol of fertility and birth, has always been
closely associated with women. It was the
symbol of maternity. In consequence of this
connection, it is urged by Elliot Smith, the
men of the Upper Palæolithic Age came in time
to conceive of the cowrie as a Great Mother, and
to give expression to their new ideas by turning
the shell into a woman, by adding to the shell
arms, legs and a trunk and head, thus producing
a grotesque feminine image, formed of the combination of a woman and a shell (12). Since
the earliest known feminine images, those of
the Aurignacian, one of which is depicted in
the Plate, do not seem to bear this shell character, it is possible that the Great Mother
first took shape as a woman with the maternal

parts greatly exaggerated, and that this idea became fused later on with the idea of the shell, thus producing the later type of image that has definite shell associations, instances of which are to be found in the frontispiece of this book. Which explanation be the true one, there is no doubt of the intimate connection between the Great Mother and shells.

Once the conception of a Great Mother had arisen, *Religion* was in the making, although in these early stages it had but few of the features that characterize it nowadays. The Great Mother was at first but little more than an amulet. Nevertheless she was, as Elliot Smith insists, the first deity that man turned to for consolation and protection from the manifold dangers of this mortal life.

The Great Mother soon began to live a life of her own, and to acquire new characteristics. Not only did she exist in the " food-gathering " days of the Palæolithic Age, in the times when men had not yet learned to produce food by artificial means ; but she survived into the earliest food-producing civilizations of the earth of which we have knowledge. For images like those of the Upper Palæolithic Age are found in pre-dynastic graves in Egypt, and in the earliest sites in Crete, the Ægean, Greece, Asia Minor, Elam, Mesopotamia, Bosnia, the Danube valley, South Russia and Malta, but especially in Egypt and the eastern Mediterranean—that is to say, in the first known civilization (13). No such images have been found in the outlying parts of the earth, such as India, Oceania, America and the southern part of Africa, where the date of appearance of civilization is much later. The Great Mother is at home in the region where, in historical times, mother goddesses played so important a part in religious systems. Curiously enough, traces of feminine images of this type die out at the end of the Stone Age in France and other parts of western Europe. This is because the centre of gravity of civilization shifted, with the coming of food-production, to the eastern Mediterranean, and remained there for many centuries.

The possible derivation of the idea of the Great Mother from a shell lends interest to the close association, in later times, between her and all the givers of life that were derived from shells. Aphrodite, the Greek goddess, was connected with Cyprus, and with the cowrie shell, itself called *Cyprœa* from its connection with that island. In Greek art Aphrodite is sometimes represented emerging from a pearl shell, showing that she had come into relationship with another giver of life, Margarita, which name itself means " giver of life." When the spider shell of the Red Sea came into the orbit, and ultimately gave rise to the connection between the octopus and the fertilizing power of water, the mother goddess became linked up with the octopus. In like manner, the mother goddess of Egypt, Hathor, enters into combination with various

givers of life. The earliest Egyptian hieroglyphic sign for gold was a necklace of golden
cowrie shells. This emblem became the deter-
minative for Hathor, the Golden Hathor, the
Lady of Nubia, the land whence came the
gold. She was also connected with Punt, the
place whence, at later times, the Egyptians
derived so many life-giving substances for use
in their temple ritual. She was the Lady
of Turquoise, and connected with the Sinaitic
Peninsula, where the Egyptians got their turquoise, which was regarded by them as a giver
of life.

The preoccupation of mankind with its
nourishment caused the Great Mother, at an
early stage of development of civilization, to
come into intimate relationship with the various
sources of food-supply. Mothers feed their
children with milk : therefore, in early times, in
Egypt, when cows had been domesticated,
new ideas were acquired, and the cow was
regarded as a form of the Great Mother, because
she also feeds children with her milk. The
Great Mother, on the other hand, was provided
with cow's horns, and was called, on certain
occasions, the Divine Cow. The idea of milk
as food for man influenced early thought profoundly in other directions, as Mr. Donald
Mackenzie has shown (14). The sap of trees
was supposed to be milk ; and such trees
and plants as came into prominence for this
reason were closely connected with the mother
goddess ; for instance, the cedar, incense trees,

sycamore, bryony, mandrake, lotus, and other plants that resemble them.

The complications that grew up around the idea of the Great Mother are seemingly endless. She was not only life-giving and beneficent, but she was also destructive. This destructiveness was not towards those whom she protects, but towards their enemies. As protector she destroyed enemies and warded off danger. This idea evidently was related to the practice of wearing necklaces of the teeth and claws of dangerous animals; for, in food-producing communities, the Great Mother was a protector, and in this connection was closely associated with dangerous animals. Thus, Upper and Lower Egypt each had a protecting mother goddess, and a protecting animal, closely connected with her, the vulture for Upper Egypt and the uræus (the poisonous asp) for Lower Egypt. The Great Mother thus came to be identified with two distinct sets of animals, the milk-giving horned cow, and, by a process of transmission, other horned animals such as the gazelle and the deer; and with dangerous beasts of prey. In one aspect she fed men; in another she protected them.

The periodicity of women caused the Great Mother to be connected with the moon, so that all early mother goddesses were moon goddesses. Women gave birth to children. Therefore, because the act of birth was like the emergence from a portal, the act of going through a gate was regarded as symbolizing birth; and the mother goddess, for instance, Artemis in Greece, was the guardian of the portal, as well as a helper in child-birth. In short, all the life-giving activities of women were reflected in the life-giving attributes of the mother goddess.

It can be said, in general, that as civilization developed, and the people acquired fresh ideas about givers of life, the Great Mother, as the great life-giver, came to be associated with each new development. In herself and her attributes she reflects the increasing complexity of early thought. The different creative crafts played an important part in the production of early ideas of creation. The potter created pots, so the creation of man could be regarded as the work of a potter; also of a carpenter, or a metal-worker. Thus we find, in Babylonia, for instance, that the mother goddess, the earliest producer of men, has such titles as " The Mother of the Gods "; " The Builder of all that has Breath "; " The Carpenter of Mankind "; " The Coppersmith of the Gods "; " The Coppersmith of the Land "; " The Lady Potter."

The civilizations of Egypt, Sumer and Elam, the earliest of which we have definite knowledge, were founded on irrigation. When this practice was begun, man realized the part played by water in the production of life, if they had not realized it before, and they elevated water to a high rank among givers of life. The combination of ideas centering round water with those centering round pottery-making, combined in a remarkable idea concerning the nature of procreation that the early Egyptians possessed. Elliot Smith says—speaking of the invention of irrigation :—" When this event happened a new view developed in explanation of the part played by woman in reproduction. She was no longer regarded as the real parent of mankind, but as the matrix in which the seed was planted and nurtured during the course of its growth and development. Hence in the earliest Egyptian hieroglyphic writing the picture of a pot of water was taken as the symbol of womanhood, the ' vessel' which received the seed. A globular water-pot, the common phonetic value of which is Nw or Nu, was the symbol of the cosmic waters, the god Nw (Nu), whose female counterpart was the goddess Nut." The idea of the water-pot has found expression in early art, for many vessels have been found, in the sites of the earliest civilization, that obviously express the relationship between women and pots, as may be seen from the example reproduced in the frontispiece. The combination of ideas concerning water and pottery-making as a creative craft thus influenced early thought profoundly, and caused men radically to modify their ideas of the nature of birth, for it became possible to regard women as " mother-pots " into which embryo children could be placed in order to grow. This, as will be seen later (see pp. 42, 146), caused the Egyptians and other people to possess curious ideas concerning the nature of conception.

The discovery of irrigation had another result of profound importance for early man. The earliest cereals grown by the Egyptians were barley and millet. Elliot Smith has suggested that the shape of the barley grain, being similar to that of the cowrie shell, and therefore to the external organ of generation, has helped to cause barley to be regarded as a form of the Great Mother, and to be possessed of life. Hence has arisen the idea of the Corn Mother, which is so widespread throughout the world, as may be seen from a perusal of Sir James Frazer's *Spirits of the Corn and the Wild*. The Japanese Shinto texts explicitly state this resemblance in the case of such cereals as rice, and such fruits as the apricot and peach (15). This doubtless accounts, likewise, in some measure, for the great importance attached, in Babylonia, to the date, for the stone of the fruit is of similar shape. The early Egyptians regarded beer as a sacred drink. Since it was made from barley, it is evident that a drink made of a life-giving substance would itself be life-giving. Thus it comes about that early agriculture was intimately bound up, for several reasons, with life-giving ideas, and that the Great Mother played an important part in agricultural ceremonies, which have always been an important feature of religious systems.

As a consequence of the association of the

Great Mother with all the new ideas that were elaborated concerning creation, and life in general, she became differentiated into numberless beings, each with some one or more distinctive attributes, just as the communities of the Roman Catholic Church have their local Madonnas. But, just as all Madonnas are derived from one prototype, so it is found that all the mother goddesses of Sumer, Egypt, and elsewhere can be equated one to the other.

CHAPTER II

GODS AND KINGS

IF the Great Mother was the first " deity " that man thought of, how are we to account for gods ? The answer to this question involves an understanding of the nature of early civilization, for gods do not seem to make their entry on the scene until the step had been taken from the food-gathering to the food-producing stage of culture, until, that is, men had definitely set their feet on the road to civilization as we know it.

The first known civilization appeared in the region called the Ancient East, which includes Egypt, the eastern Mediterranean, Asia Minor, Mesopotamia and Elam. Throughout this region are found grotesque images of the Great Mother in conjunction with these early food-producing communities.

It is important to know exactly where the step from food-gathering to food-producing took place. All the evidence goes to show that this happened in Egypt. The early civilizations of Egypt, Elam and Sumer were founded on irrigation, certainly the earliest form of food-production known to man, for tillage of the soil for dry cultivation was later than irrigation in all parts of the world. The Nile irrigation cycle is perfect, in that it is capable, without help, of growing food for man; and this is the case with no other river in the world (1). Egypt, moreover, was inhabited in Palæolithic times, and the culture of the pre-dynastic Egyptians shows signs of derivation from that of the Old Stone Age. In Egypt the growth of civilization can be watched from one stage to another, beginning with a condition similar to that of palæolithic man, and culminating in the Pyramid Age : in no other country can a like continuous progression be witnessed.

All the known evidence goes to show that the other early communities of the civilization of the Ancient East derived their culture, directly or indirectly, from Egypt of the pre-dynastic or early dynastic age. It is impossible to produce any solid body of evidence to show that any other community had influenced the culture of Egypt in those times to any appreciable extent. The hypothesis that best fits the facts is that the Egyptians, having learned the craft of irrigation, and having come to need such materials as copper, emery and so forth for their industries, began to send out expeditions to get these materials, to Elam, Turkestan, the Ægean and elsewhere, and thus in time caused their civilization to be transplanted to new homes; so that, ultimately, there was distributed through a limited area round the eastern Mediterranean a civilization of uniform nature, the culture of one community only differing from that of another in secondary details.

Although Egypt seems to have been the great pioneer country of antiquity, and in thought and culture was always on a higher level than her contemporaries, it is, in fact, in Sumer that the clearest ideas can be gained of the manner in which early men began to elaborate their notions of gods, for the clay tablets with Sumerian cuneiform inscriptions have survived the Egyptian papyri. The work of students of Sumerian culture, the late L. W. King, Professor Langdon, A. Poebel and others, have thrown a flood of light on early conditions (2). They have shown that from the earliest times there existed a number of city states, each with a ruler, and each protected by a god. The earliest known city was Eridu, the guardian deity of which was Enki. This god had many qualities associated with the Great Mother, and there can be little doubt that he was simply her male counterpart. We find that the Great Mother acquired many functions and attributes as civilization became more complex; she became a potter goddess, a snake goddess, and so forth. For some reason, some of these variations of the Great Mother changed their sex and became gods. This may sound strange; but a like transformation has demonstrably taken place in later times, as may be seen from a perusal of Barton's *Semitic Origins*. It is probable that the Great Mother was the first protecting deity of early communities ; and she was regarded, while fulfilling this function, as adopting an animal form. This may be seen in Egypt, where Upper and Lower Egypt both had their protecting goddesses, connected respectively with the vulture and the deadly asp. So, when the transformation took place from mother goddesses to gods, it is not surprising to find that these gods had animal associations and characteristics, and that these characteristics and associations have persisted for many centuries in all parts of the world. Enki, the god of Eridu in Sumer, was ram-headed, and he probably derived this feature from the fact that the Great Mother was connected with animals, or even from the resemblance between his horns and an ammonite shell, a form of giver of life closely connected with the Great Mother.

The early gods of cities are said, in Sumerian texts, to have created men and kings to carry on their cults, and to have taught them the manner of building temples. We are not told of any direct relationship between the gods and the early kings, except that the king is under the protection of the god. But it has long been known that the mother goddess of the Ancient East was accompanied, in her later manifestations, by a son and lover, who shared many of her attributes. He differed in one important respect from the mother goddess, being connected intimately with irrigation, and with agriculture and vegetation generally ; whereas the mother goddess was not concerned directly with irrigation. It is extremely important to know what caused the appearance of a " god " in connection with the mother goddess, and why he should be associated so closely with the craft on which the early civilizations were founded. In order to solve the problem it is necessary to know more of this son of the Great Mother.

In Sumer the son of the Great Mother is remembered by the name of Tammuz. He is not a product of speculation, but has been identified with a prehistoric king. In fact, it was customary to regard the early kings of Sumer as the sons of the Great Mother. Tammuz was remembered as a being who, having been drowned, was reanimated by his mother. It was formerly thought that this tradition had some reference to the annual cycle of the growth and decay of vegetation. But, as has been shown by Sir James Frazer and others, the drama of the drowning of the king must actually have taken place in Sumer. There is every reason to believe that, throughout the Ancient East, the earliest kings, who ruled over civilizations with cults of the Great Mother, in which the king was believed to be her son, were put to death, either after a certain period, or when they were old. The practice still survives in out-of-the-way places like the Upper Nile. The theory was that these kings maintained, by their own vigour, the health and fertility of

the country. Being sons of the Great Mother,
they presumably had some of her characteristics, and thus were givers of life to the community. So, when they got old they were
useless, and were put out of the way ; though
it is not clear why it was considered necessary
that they should be sacrificed.

Having identified the son of the Great Mother
with the early kings of Sumer and elsewhere,
it is now necessary to ask how the kingship
itself came into being, and why it should
apparently be so closely associated with irrigation. Inquiry shows at once that the early
kings of Egypt and Sumer were especially
connected with the irrigation systems of those
countries. One of the earliest Egyptian pictures represents a king cutting the first sod of
an irrigation canal, and the greatest benefit a
king could confer on his subjects was that of
maintaining the irrigation system. The close
association between early kings and irrigation
systems suggests that the beginning of ruling
class was in some way bound up with that of
irrigation (3). The elaboration of the irrigation
system in Egypt was certainly gradual, and no
reason exists to suggest that a group of the
community came into power in that connection. In Egypt, with the annual flood of
the Nile, it must have been difficult for the
agriculturist, without some method of count-
ing time, to know exactly when to begin oper-
ations. The day of the beginning of the flood
was of great importance to him, for his work

must cease once the water had begun to flow
over the land. Thus it is that the day of the
flood was the beginning of the Egyptian year.
The Egyptians measured all their time from
that date. The calculation of the recurrence
of such a day as that of the Nile flood is not
easy. It involves the use of a calendar based
on the movements of some heavenly body.
The Egyptians used, in the first instance, the
lunar calendar in order to calculate this important date. The royal family was closely interested in calendrical matters ; for, in the early
royal inscriptions, mention is made constantly
of the height of the Nile. In Babylonia a
like preoccupation is evident, for the royal
astronomers made a daily report to the king
of the position of the heavenly bodies. The
whole of the agricultural ritual of the early
civilizations, with which ritual the ruling family
was closely bound up, was based on the calendar.
It is impossible, also, to dissociate early ruling
groups and calendars. Since the knowledge
of the calendar must be ascribed to the genius
of some man, it seems reasonable to believe
that the inventor of the lunar calendar was
the ancestor of the first ruling group in the
world. A sudden stroke of genius, in a matter
that directly concerns the welfare of the whole
community, can well explain the rise of one
family to a position of privilege (4).

Given the origin of the ruling group, how
came the early kings to be connected with the
idea of a god ? Such beings as Tammuz,

Attis and Adonis can hardly be called gods, though they are on the way to that goal: they are too human; they represent rather a tradition of the days when kings were sacrificed for the good of the community. The most important development in the idea of a god seems to have taken place in Egypt, in connection with Osiris, who, although presenting many signs of similarity to Tammuz, is markedly different in some respects (5). Osiris, like Tammuz, was regarded as a former king, but he was always spoken of as a dead king. The actual king of Egypt, in dynastic times, personated Horus, the son of Osiris. When the king died he was identified with Osiris, and, as Osiris, ruled over the land of the dead. Osiris certainly corresponds to current ideas of "deity": he was a spirit; he existed somewhere else as a spirit, but, at the same time, in communication with men. In this he contrasts with Tammuz, who is simply said to have died and come to life again. The reason for this difference apparently lies in the fact that Osiris was, in Egypt, connected with mummification, a practice that certainly was invented by the Egyptians; he is always represented as a mummy, whereas Tammuz is never represented in art at all. The aim of mummification was the securance of immortality. The Egyptians regarded immortality in terms of the body; and they believed that anyone who had been embalmed, and had families who could ensure the performance of the necessary ritual, was assured of eternal life in the land of the dead ruled by Osiris, by virtue of the fact that, by the act of mummification itself, he was identified with Osiris, the first king who died.

The coming into being of the practice of mummification, and of ideas of the persistence of the dead in another place, caused the king of Egypt to be regarded as Horus, the son of Osiris. The living king was charged with the maintenance of the cults attaching to his dead father. He provided him with food, which was necessary for him to remain alive in the other world. The king also performed the ritual necessary to reanimate the body of his father, or his portrait statue, in order that the dead king might partake of the food, and hold communication with the living. This cult may thus be regarded as an ancestor-cult, or as a cult of a god, according to the point of view. Osiris was the father of the man who carried on his cult ; he also was the king who conferred benefits on the whole community. Hence the dual aspect of the cult. Therefore, in the cult of Osiris, we see the beginning of the worship, not only of gods, but also of ancestors. As Elliot Smith says :— " Osiris was the prototype of all gods ; his ritual was the basis of all religious ceremonial ; his priests who conducted the animating ceremonies were the pioneers of a long series of ministers who for more than fifty centuries, in spite of the endless variety of details of their ritual and the character of their temples, have continued to perform ceremonies that have undergone remarkably little essential change "(6). The Egyptians claimed that all funerary cults originated with Osiris, that he gave them their religious doctrines, their rites, the rules for their sanctuaries and plans for their temples.

The early ideas that the Egyptians had about kings and gods were not allowed to remain unaltered. For, in process of time, a new development of thought worked profound transformations in Egyptian life, both in religion and in politics. This new thought in all probability originated at Heliopolis, one of the nomes, or territorial divisions, of Lower Egypt (7). From the earliest known times the Heliopolitans were important in Egyptian life. Signs of their influence are found in the early dynasties, in the inclusion of the name of their great god, the sun god Re, in royal names. Their influence may also be traced in other directions. In order to explain how this influence worked, attention must be paid for a moment to the tombs used in the first dynasties by the royal family. These tombs were called mastabas. They consisted of (a) a multi-chambered subterranean grave, to which a stairway gave access ; (b) a brickwork superstructure in the shape of four walls enclosing a mass of earth or rubble ; and (c) an enclosure for offerings in front of the mastaba. These tombs were given up in the Third Dynasty by the royal family. The Third Dynasty begins the Pyramid

Age, when the kings used pyramids for their tombs. It opened with Zoser. Until his reign the mastabas were made of sun-dried brick, with, in one or two cases, a floor of limestone. Zoser built a mastaba with a burial chamber, the entrance to which was closed by portcullis stones. He then made a stone mastaba, eighty feet high, two hundred and twenty feet wide, and an uncertain amount longer from north to south. As time went on he built five others on top, each smaller than its predecessor, producing a terraced structure one hundred and ninety feet high, in six stages, like the Babylonian ziggurat or stepped pyramid. This is the first large stone structure known to history, and in shape it approximates to a pyramid. The next royal tomb was a pyramid, and thenceforth for many centuries the pyramid was the royal tomb.

The ideas expressed in the pyramids and the mastaba tombs are essentially different. The nobility continued for several dynasties to be buried in mastabas; and these tombs, as would be expected, contain references to the deities of the early dynasties, Osiris, Hathor and the rest. The pyramids, on the other hand, contain a solar theology, something that had not hitherto appeared on royal tombs. It is true that the texts all date from the pyramids of the Fifth and Sixth Dynasties, when the solar theology had become predominant in Egypt; but the inference is that the pyramid was always associated with solar ideas. In any case, the pyramids and mastabas of the Fifth and Sixth Dynasties present a complete contrast in ideas.

How came it that the royal family, in adopting a new form of tomb, also adopted a new theology? The answer is that the Heliopolitans evidently were influencing the thought of the royal family, and were exerting a pressure that was destined ultimately to land them on the throne.

Why should the coming of the sun-cult be such a remarkable event in Egypt? It is often thought to be perfectly natural for men to worship the sun, since it is the source of light and life. The yearly recurrence of vegetation would, it might be argued, have caused men to pay close attention to the sun. But this is not the case. It can be shown that the sun-cult has not arisen spontaneously in all parts of the world; that, on the contrary, as will be shown in Chapter VI, it only persists in certain circumstances. The ancient Egyptians in the beginning ascribed the fertility of their land, not to the sun, but to the Nile flood, and more or less rightly; and they even went so far as to believe that the green waters of the Nile made the vegetation green. For them the sun had nothing whatever to do with the process.

The sun-cult in Egypt was at first confined to Heliopolis. Of that there is no reasonable doubt. So, in thinking of the origin of the sun-cult, search must be made for something

that marks Heliopolis off from the rest of
Egypt. This is readily found in the fact
that the solar calendar was invented there.
The Egyptians, once they had discovered the
craft of irrigation, needed to know the date
of the flood of the Nile, which begins each year
on or about the same day. For this end the
lunar calendar was invented, and this calendar
was, as has been seen, connected with the
ruling family. The lunar calendar is a clumsy
instrument for calculating dates, as anyone
knows who tries to work out the date of Easter
for any year. So the solar calendar, or rather
the Sothic calendar, based on the movements
of Sirius, which the Egyptians called Sothis,
once invented, would easily displace the older
and clumsier instrument for the purpose of
measuring time. It has been calculated, from
astronomical evidence, that this calendar must
have been invented at Heliopolis. Heliopolis
was also unique in ancient Egypt, for it was the
place where the first Nilometer was made:
the markings on all other Nilometers were
calculated from that of Heliopolis.

The solar calendar coincides almost exactly
with the Sothic calendar (that based on Sirius).
It is therefore likely that men who were engaged
in making observations of the movements of
Sirius would soon begin to pay attention to
the sun, and, once that had happened, the
elaboration of a solar theology could easily
follow. The god of Heliopolis, Re, was evidently a product of speculation, for he bears

no signs of having been, like Osiris, a king. He was born on New Year's Day, the day of the Nile flood ; he was born out of the primeval ocean, which may mean the flood of the Nile, or the mother goddess Nut ; he came out of an egg made by Khnum, the potter god ; he was lifted, on the back of Nut, in the form of the Great Cow, one of the forms of the Great Mother, to the sky, where he is born of her every day. Thus he was pieced together from elements of thought already existing in Egypt, and in no way seems to be historical, as was Osiris.

The Heliopolitans were responsible for the invention of the idea of a world in the sky, where kings could live eternally in the company of the gods. This idea is quite foreign to the earlier, Osirian, theology. The preference shown by the kings of the Fifth and Sixth Dynasties for the sky-world is a sign of its greater attractiveness ; and the inference is that this feature of Heliopolitan theology was eagerly seized on by the kings of the early dynasties, and that this predilection caused the kings to include Re in their names as a sign of their attachment to him and his world.

The Heliopolitans seem to have performed another great service for the ruling family. In a story called The Destruction of Mankind, it is recorded how Re, when old, became angry because his subjects murmured against him, presumably because he ought to have been sacrificed (8). He called a council of the gods, who advise him to slay the conspirators. Accordingly he got Hathor, the mother goddess, his " Eye," to kill men. She did so in her Sekhmet, or lioness, aspect. Unfortunately, once she began to kill men, she did not want to stop, and Re became alarmed. He sent messengers to Elephantine, the First Cataract, to get a red substance, and this, mixed with beer, was poured on the ground during the night. When the goddess came in the morning to kill the survivors, she found the beer, and drank so much that she was unable any longer to recognize men, and thus the rest were saved. This story is the prototype of that widespread group of tales of a great destruction of men, whether by flood, fire, or some other means, which occur, for instance, in Genesis, in the form of the stories of the flood and of the destruction of Sodom and Gomorrah. But we are not now concerned with the story as a whole. The point of interest at present is that Re, the god, was not killed, like Osiris, or Tammuz, when he was old. He was not regarded as a dead king, but as a living king, who, having become old, is rejuvenated by the blood of his people. Evidently the Heliopolitans had argued that the blood of a victim would rejuvenate the king, that the king need not be killed when he became old, and thereby had placed the kingship on an entirely different footing. Henceforth the king had power over his subjects, and was no longer forced to sacrifice himself for the good of the community. It is in this episode that many of the troubles of mankind probably take their origin. For, from the practice of offering slaves as human sacrifices instead of the king, the custom of warfare evidently developed, and ruling groups have gradually educated themselves in the practice of fighting. It is found, in Sumer, that when the mother goddess came to be associated with the heavenly bodies, she developed warlike qualities, which suggests that this doctrine of the Heliopolitans was spreading. The Great Mother in this respect, as in others, reflected, in her attributes, the political and social institutions of mankind.

The power of the Heliopolitan priesthood must have increased enormously as the result of the introduction of this reform in sacrifice. But, in spite of their contributions to the welfare of the community, and to the prestige of the ruling group, they could not yet attain to the heights that they reached in the Fifth Dynasty, when they secured the throne. The reason for this is bound up with the foundation of the royal family. Every king personified Horus, the son of Osiris, and, in the early dynasties, each king was probably related to his predecessor. Re himself never was a king on earth—at least there is no evidence for that assumption—and he had, at first, no son as king. Also the cult of the royal family was centred round Osiris, with whom every king was identified after death. The Heliopolitans therefore, intent, as they probably were, on gaining power, were faced with the problem of making Re the father of a man, and of getting the royal family to believe this story. This they evidently succeeded in doing, for the Fifth Dynasty included kings calling themselves *Sons of the Sun,* and ever after the Pharaoh has borne this title.

How was this feat accomplished ? Apparently by one of the craftiest pieces of reasoning ever perpetrated. The story goes that Khufu, the great king of the Fourth Dynasty, was enjoying an idle hour with his sons, while they narrated wonders wrought by the great wise men of old. When, thereupon, Prince Harzozef told the king that there still lived a magician able to do marvels of the same kind, the Pharaoh sent the prince to fetch the wise man. The latter, after he had offered some examples of his remarkable powers, reluctantly told the king in response to questions, that the three children to be born by the wife of a certain priest of Re were begotten of Re himself, and that they would all become kings of Egypt. This happened, and thereby was produced one of the most important events in the history of mankind.

Let us see how the Heliopolitans went to work to explain this form of birth. Full accounts are not available until the Eighteenth Dynasty, when the manner of birth of Queen Hatshepsut is described (9). The story of her birth falls into two parts. In one case the god, Re, personates the king, and has intercourse with

the queen. That being done, he then gets
Khnum, the potter god, to make for him, on
his potter's wheel, two embryo children, representing the child and its ka, or double, which
are to be placed in the queen to be born in
the usual manner. This evidently is based on
the idea that a woman is a mother pot, into
which seed can be placed to grow. Khnum
therefore takes part in the formation of Re
himself, and also of his children. So Re was
not really, according to this version, the father
of the king. Presumably this story gained the
throne for the family of Heliopolis. The coming to power of the Heliopolitan ruling family
produced an entirely new situation in Egypt.
The king, as Son of the Sun, was now the
actual son of a living deity, he was a demi-
god, and not, as in the case of the earlier kings,
the son of a dead king. The father of the
king was the god of the living, not of the
dead.

By their accession to power the Heliopolitans
split the ruling group of Egypt into two parts.
The ruling family were connected with the
sky, and with the sun god; the older ruling
group, together with the nobility, were still
connected with Osiris, and went after death
to his otherworld. By this act the Children of
the Sun split the ruling power of Egypt, and
sowed the seeds of future weakness (10). But
the solar theology soon had to compromise with
the older, deeper-seated Osirian theology. In
course of time Osiris was elevated to the sky

world, there to rule over the dead, and to
become inextricably mixed with Re, the sun
god. It is only when the sun-cult was first
instituted as the state cult of Egypt that the
distinction between the two theologies is at all
sharp.

With the coming to power of the Children of
the Sun the kingship reached a height in Egypt
that it never attained in any other country.
The king had royal names to signify his kingship, and even identity, with the gods. He
was called Horus, to make him son of the
gods ; and along with this name went two
titles, the name of the ka, or double, and the
Golden Horus name. The Golden Horus name
was to show his divine origin. Along with
this name went variable epithets descriptive of
each king. By virtue of the Horus name the
king acquired the soul and body of Horus
himself. He also had solar names, to signify
his birth from the sun god, and these names
made him Re incarnate. The king was given
the fluid of Re, the gold of the gods and goddesses, which fluid he was able to transmit to
his son, the crown prince, who was associated
with him on the throne.

The king at his coronation was also invested
with the regalia, with material givers of life,
which served to protect him. The main function of Egyptian kings was to maintain the cult
of the gods. This cult, as in the case of the
Osiris cult, was still an ancestor-cult. As
Son of the Sun, the king of Egypt had to carry

on a cult connected with his father in a sanctuary
called the House of the Morning, attached to the
Heliopolitan temple of the sun. He had to rise
at dawn, and, after purifying himself, perform the daily temple liturgy by washing or
sprinkling the sun god's image, imitating thereby the daily regenerative lustration undergone
by that god before he appeared above the
horizon. The king was washed with water,
and fumigated with incense. He also chewed
natron, and thus became fit to chant the
praises of the god. He was then robed, anointed
and decked with insignia, all of them givers
of life, and then proceeded to perform a similar
toilet for the image of the sun god. Thus
it is patent that the time of the king must
have been largely occupied with religious
ceremonial.

Between the times when the Great Mother
was the sole being who could be regarded as a
deity, and the times when the King of Egypt
was an incarnate deity, the son of the sun god,
there exists a great contrast. Thought had
gone a long way to the development of ideas
that are purely religious, ideas that, if their
history were not known fairly well, would
suggest an inborn faculty of man for the elaboration of purely religious beliefs directly from
the contemplation of nature. When we follow
in the footsteps of the priests of Heliopolis,
we have planted our feet firmly on the path
that leads to the great monotheistic religions

of antiquity, all of which seem to derive their inspiration from the speculations of these remarkable men. The religious beliefs of the kings of the Eighteenth Dynasty of Egypt, of Zoroaster of Persia, of the Brahmins of India, and last, but not least, of the prophets of Israel, bear witness to the influence of this current of thought. Man's ideas, by the elaboration of the sun-cult, were turned from the earth to the heavens, where he was henceforth to look for the great Creator and Preserver of the universe. But man had to build a scaffolding of thought to enable him to reach the skies : he did not leap there, even in thought, at one bound.

CHAPTER III

EARLY IDEAS ABOUT DEATH

T HE men of the caves in western Europe buried their dead in a crouching position, often packed round with red ochre. This position has been interpreted in two ways : it is said by some to be the attitude of sleep ; so that, since death evidently was thought in those times to be a sleep, the body was put in that posture. On the other hand, it is urged that, man being born of the Great Mother, whose images were found in those caves, he was returned to her in the position he occupied before birth.

The contracted mode of disposal of the dead has had a long and widespread vogue, it being characteristic of the early food-producing communities, as well as of many existing food-producing peoples of the lower culture. In pre-dynastic Egypt the dead were buried, in a crouching position, in shallow graves dug in the hot dry sand, and this custom persisted among the commoners for many centuries after the ruling classes had adopted other modes of burial (1). In pre-dynastic Egyptian

46

burials the body was protected from the soil
by linen, mats or skins, sometimes even by
sticks, or by a wooden frame in the grave.
The graves, at first quite shallow, gradually
developed, as the wealth of the country increased,
and some of them became large rectangular
pits. At the end of the pre-dynastic period
in Egypt, which, according to the dating of
Meyer, occured about 3300 B.C., some of the
large graves were lined with brickwork to
prevent the sand from falling in ; and were
supplied with roofs of branches, or of logs
with bricks on them, or corbel vaults made of
mud brick. In the course of time these graves
developed into regular underground dwellings,
with suites of rooms. This shows that the
ghost of the dead was supposed to live in the
tomb ; and this idea never seems to have
been lost by the Egyptians, Sumerians, and
other peoples. The underground tomb seems
to have led to the idea that the dead lived
in an underworld, where, according to Sumerian
ideas, the dead were sunk in deep sleep.

One of the most important ideas associated
with death is that of immortality. The two
oldest known civilizations, those of Egypt
and Sumer, differed profoundly in regard to
conceptions of life after death. The Sumerians,
and the Babylonians after them, had no idea
of immortality ; the most they could hope for
was long life and good health (2). The gift of
life after death was in the hands of the gods,
and men had not succeeded in wresting it from

them. It was left for the Egyptians to formulate, and to develop, ideas with regard to a conscious life in the hereafter.

In pre-dynastic times, in Egypt, the dead, buried in the hot dry sand, were often marvellously preserved. When burial practices became more complicated, and the wealthy began to place their dead in coffins of various sorts, the bodies decayed. This, Elliot Smith claims, caused the Egyptians to begin to take measures to counteract this process, and ultimately to develop their wonderful craft of mummification. Mummification began in the First Dynasty, so far as is known, and the first good examples date from the Second Dynasty. The aim of the practice was to preserve the body, as intact as possible, in its outward form, and in the likeness of the dead as he was in life. To do this the Egyptians invented detail after detail of technique, and experimented with substance after substance. In the early mummies attempts were made to mould the features of the deceased, and sometimes death masks were made. But the most important development was that connected with the making of portrait statues of the dead, wonderful examples of the sculptor's art, which betray the desire of the Egyptians to preserve the likeness of their departed. The making of these statues caused a revolution in tomb construction. At first the grave only had subterranean chambers, which contained the body. With the making of portrait statues,

there developed the "statue-house" in the part
of the tomb that was above ground, and a
chapel where offerings of food were made to
the statue, in which chapel the living held
communication with the dead. Thus the
mastaba came into existence. The Egyptians
also, in their early attempts, sometimes placed
portrait heads of the deceased in the grave
along with the body, but they never did this
when they made a statue.

The making of portrait statues evidently
had great effects on the minds of the Egyptians.
" All these varied experiments were inspired
by the same desire, to preserve the likeness of
the deceased. But when the sculptors attained
their object, and created those marvellous
life-like portraits, which must ever remain
marvels of technical skill and artistic feeling,
the old ideas that surged through the minds
of the pre-dynastic Egyptians as they con-
templated the desiccated remains of the dead,
were strongly reinforced. The earlier people's
thoughts were turned more especially than
heretofore to the contemplation of the nature
of life and death, by seeing the bodies of their
dead preserved whole and incorruptible; and,
if their actions can be regarded as an expression
of their ideas, they began to wonder what
was lacking in these physically complete bodies
to prevent them from feeling and acting like
living beings. Such must have been the results
of their puzzled contemplation of the great
problems of life and death. Otherwise the

impulse to make more certain the preservation
of the body of the deceased by means of a
sculptured statue remains inexplicable. But
when the corpse had been rendered incorruptible
and the deceased's portrait had been fashioned
with realistic perfection, the old ideas would
recur with renewed strength. The belief then
took more definite shape that if the missing
elements of vitality could be restored to the
statue, it might become animated and the dead
man would live again in his vitalized statue.
This prompted a more intense and searching
investigation of the problems concerning the
nature of the elements of vitality of which
the corpse was deprived at the time of death.
Out of these inquiries in course of time a highly
complex system of philosophy developed " (3).
In fact, the Egyptians came to believe that they
could keep the dead alive in the other world,
that they could procure " Immortality " for the
dead.

The idea of " Immortality " grew up, in
Egypt, round the ritual of mummification.
This idea was not that of the immortality of
the soul as we conceive it, but rather of the
body itself. This is made clear by the following quotation from Breasted's *Development of
Religion and Thought in Ancient Egypt*:—" It
is evident that the Egyptians never wholly
dissociated a person from the body as an
instrument or vehicle of sensation, and they
resorted to elaborate devices to restore to
the body its various channels of sensibility,

after the ba, which comprehended these very things, had detached itself from the body." The dead had, as it were, to be reborn. Then, and then only, did they exist as " souls," dependent on the good offices of the living for their sustenance, which made the funerary ritual so important. When the dead had become " souls," they could subsist and survive in the life hereafter. As Breasted remarks: " It is not correct to attribute to the Egyptians a belief in the *immortality* of the soul strictly interpreted as imperishability or to speak of his ' ideas of immortality," (4). The Egyptians simply believed that the dead could be brought to life, and thus enabled to live, in another world, through the offices of the living, as carried out in the funerary ritual. Osiris, who is so directly associated with mummification, was said by the Egyptians to have been the first king who died. That is to say, he was the first man to undergo the process of death and rebirth, which leads to " immortality," to a new life in another place. Thus arose, in Egypt, the conception of death and rebirth as the prelude to immortality. In the beginning the idea was crude, and dealt with the actual death and rebirth of the physical body, with all its attributes. But in the end the idea became refined, it lost its physical connotations, and came to refer to the life of the spirit. This idea has been one of the most potent in the formation and in the perpetuation of religious systems that the world has known.

It must never be forgotten that the ritual of mummification was closely connected with Osiris, the dead king, who ruled in the other world. As Elliot Smith suggests, the desire to keep a king alive as long as possible may have had a great effect in driving the Egyptians towards the elaboration of their craft of mummification. At first mummification was confined to kings, and every king that was mummified was believed to become one with Osiris, and, as Osiris, to rule over the dead. He was, at the same time, living in the tomb, and his portrait statue could be animated when necessary. In order to animate portrait statues a ritual procedure was resorted to, which was of a threefold nature. First libations were poured out, then incense was burned, and finally came the operation of opening of the mouth, by which the breath of life was imparted to the statue. Dr. A. M. Blackman has shown, from the Pyramid Texts, what was the significance of this ritual. He shows that the meaning conveyed by the texts is that the deceased has lost his bodily fluids and odours, and that they must be restored to him. " These thy libations, Osiris—These thy libations, O Unas, which have come forth before thy son, which have come forth before Horus. I have come I have brought to thee the Horus-eye that thy heart may be cool possessing it." Again : " The offering of libations. The water belongs to thee, the flood belongs to thee, the fluid that issued from the god, the exudation

that issued from Osiris." A later text mentions
incense: "The grains of incense are the exuda-
tions of a divinity, the fluid which issued from
his flesh, the god's sweat descending to the
ground." Blackman says:—"The general
meaning of these passages is quite clear. The
corpse of the deceased is dry and shrivelled.
To revivify it the vital fluids that have exuded
from it must be restored, for not till then
will life return and the heart beat again. This,
so the texts show us, was believed to be accompanied by offering libations to the accompani-
ment of incantations" (5).

The animation of the portrait statue was
not complete until the chief ceremony had been
accomplished, that of *The Opening of the Mouth*.
This was performed by touching, with a copper
chisel, the mouth, ears, eyes and nose of the
statue, after which it was really supposed to live.

The ritual of mummification, and the making
of portrait statues, depended on the use of
"givers of life." In the ritual of the death
and resurrection of Osiris, the prototype of
funeral ceremonies, the mummy is decked with
amulets of lapis lazuli, malachite and electrum,
and is placed on a boat in a cabin made of
sycamore and acacia woods, both of which
woods are "life-giving." In the actual ceremony of animation of the portrait statue, use
is made of "the great magician," a serpent-
shaped wand; of the adze of Anubis (the
inventor of mummification); of incense; of
pots of Nile water and of paint, all of which

are supposed to be givers of life, for reasons unconnected with mummification. In the actual process of mummification, Horus, the son of Osiris, reanimates the body by means of magical passes : the holy paints, water, oils are then used to make unctions for the eyes, mouth, ears and members of the body, which are thereby made to function (6).

The Egyptians had definite reasons for all stages in the ritual of animation of portrait statues. The use of libations was derived from ideas connected with irrigation : water was regarded as life-giving ; so the priests in charge of the ritual substituted Nile water for the fluids of decomposition which they originally offered to the portrait statue or mummy, in order to reanimate it. The resinous substances, burned as incense, were used because the deceased used them for the application of face-paints and so forth, so that by burning incense the odours of the living were being restored to him. In the course of time, when the idea of gods became developed, the burning of incense took on a different aspect. The touching of the mouth of the portrait statue with the copper chisel was a creative act, as was also the act of making the portrait statue. Dr. Alan Gardiner says : " That statues in Egypt were meant to be efficient animate substitutes for the person or creature they portrayed has not been sufficiently emphasized hitherto. Over every statue or image were performed the rites of ' opening the mouth '

—magical passes made with a kind of metal chisel in front of the mouth. Besides the *up-ro*, ' mouth-opening,' other words testify to the prevalence of the same idea ; the word for ' to fashion a statue ' (*ms*) is to all appearance identical with *ms*, ' to give birth ' (i.e. the idea of ' Giver of Life ' in another form), and the term for the sculptor was *sa'nkh*, ' he who causes to live ' '' (7).

It is significant that the chief god of Memphis, the city that played so important a part in Egypt in the time when portrait statues were first made, was Ptah, whose name apparently means " sculptor," " engraver." He was the god of handicraftsmen. Ptah is said to have made for the gods their images, their cities and the districts over which they ruled. He also placed the gods in their sanctuaries, and made their bodies. He was the lord of life, and was believed to fashion the bodies of the dead for their life in the underworld. He performed the ceremony of the opening of the mouth of the portrait statues of the gods. Thus, as in the case of pottery-making, a creative craft had a conspicuous influence on thought. The stone quarries at Troja in the Makattan mountains opposite Memphis belonged to Ptah. Thence was got all the stone for the pyramids and mastabas, and this stone was worked up by the high priests of Ptah and the workmen attached to the temple. The high priest of Ptah was the chief artificer of the kingdom.

The ritual of mummification made it imper-
ative that the family of the deceased should
enact the parts played by the family of Osiris
in the drama of his death and resurrection.
Osiris was killed and dismembered by his
brother Set, and his members were collected
and reunited by his son Horus, with the aid of
the jackal god Anubis, the god who is said to
have invented mummification.

It is significant of the universal capacity
possessed by men of holding entirely contra-
dictory beliefs, that the Egyptians, having
elaborated their ideas connected with mummification, which involved the belief that the
dead were alive in the tomb, also developed
out the idea of a land where the dead could
enjoy a life like that on earth, something quite
different from the existence in the underworld
of the Sumerians. The connection between
Osiris and a land of the dead is not quite clear.
In the beginning he is said to have gone from
Bubastis, in the Delta of the Nile, to Abydos,
in Upper Egypt, where he became ruler over
" The Westerners," thereby displacing Anubis
as god of the dead. Nevertheless, once the
Osirian ideas became current, the old notions,
whatever they were, soon disappeared, and the
Osirian dead lived a happy existence in the
Isles of the Blest, which, according to some
accounts, were situated in the Delta of the
Nile.

The idea of life in the hereafter was greatly
developed, and made more attractive, in the

solar theology. Osiris depended on the good
offices of his son for food and sustenance, and
he was ruler over the dead. But Re was a
mighty god, who could intervene in the affairs
of men, who was incarnate in the king, in
his son Horus. Re was a great creator, by
means of his rays, his voice, and the words
he uttered. Life in the sky was different
from that in the other world, and at first the
Pyramid Texts show that the kings who went
from the sky regarded themselves as rescued
from the world of Osiris. In the words of
Breasted : " The early belief that the soul
lived in or at the tomb, which must therefore
be equipped to furnish his necessities as in the
hereafter, was one from which the Egyptian
never escaped entirely, not even at the present
day." But with the development of the solar
theology comes " the emergence of a more
highly developed and more desirable hereafter,
which has gradually supplanted the older
and simpler view. The common people doubtless still thought of their dead either as dwelling
in the tomb, or at best as inhabiting the gloomy
realm of the gods eventually led by Osiris.
But for the great of the earth, the king and
his nobles at least, a happier destiny now
dawned. They might dwell at will with the
sun god in his glorious celestial kingdom. In
the royal tomb we henceforth discern the
emergence of this solar hereafter " (8). The
Pyramid Texts do not mention an underworld at all. The king goes to the sky :—

" He has freed king Teti from Kherti, he has not given him over to Osiris " : Horus " puts not this Pepi over the dead, he puts him among the gods, he being divine " (9).

CHAPTER IV

THE SEARCH FOR THE EARTHLY PARADISE

THE elaboration, by the Egyptians, of ideas connected with the life to come had tremendous consequences. It ultimately led men from the Ancient East to the uttermost ends of the earth in search of the Earthly Paradise, the place where givers of life abounded, and immortal life, together with eternal youth, were to be enjoyed. The story of this search is one of the most romantic that can be told, for the quest lasted down to within comparatively modern times, the Spaniards on their arrival in America actually sending out expeditions to find the " Fountains of Youth " that were reputed to exist in the centre of Florida.

It must not be thought that the connotation that the word paradise possesses to-day is identical with that which it possessed for the ancients. They seem actually, like the Spaniards with their Fountains of Youth, to have believed in a place on the earth where immortal life was to be enjoyed, not in some mythical region that never existed except in men's fancies, as we now know to be the case.[1] It is quite obvious that the idea of an earthly paradise, once elaborated, would prove a most potent attractive force. For what stronger incentive to adventure could be offered to mortal man ? The lure of wealth would be as nothing compared with it. The instinct of self-preservation, the desire to preserve life, and to avert death, would cause men to brave any dangers, if at the end of their search they thought that they could gain these boons in such happy surroundings.

The facts connected with the early spread of civilization throughout the world form a consistent whole, as will now be shown.

The story of the spread of civilization from its homeland in the Ancient East reveals the desire for certain substances as one of the mainsprings of human activity in former times. The earliest known civilizations, those of Egypt, Sumer, Crete and elsewhere in the Ancient East, existed about 3000 B.C., and some of them much earlier. They were all similar in culture, and were in communication with each other to a certain extent. For instance, the pre-dynastic Egyptians possessed stores of emery, which they had got from Naxos in the Cyclades Islands of the Ægean Archipelago. In this early civilization, characterized as it was by

[1] Cf. page 87, for the quotation from Ezekiel xxviii. 11 *et seq.*, where it is quite clear that the garden of Eden was regarded as an actual place.

the making of grotesque images of the Great
Mother, there does not seem to be any con-
clusive sign of a widespread search for life-
giving substances, such as is revealed in later
times : the need for homely materials, for
instance copper and so forth, seems to have
been the motive that led to the foundation
of fresh settlements in various places. At the
same time, there is evidence that, even at this
early stage, givers of life were being transported
from one place to another. As an example,
pearl-bearing oysters from the Red Sea have
been found in Italian caves of neolithic times.
But, in these early days, the idea of immortality had not yet emerged, so far as is known.
All that can be said is that the little world of
the Ancient East formed a cultural beacon in
the midst of darkness, the area illuminated by
which was gradually being widened, as men
worked their way step by step from the Mediterranean, to explore the countries to the north.
The people of the Ancient East were continually
elaborating fresh needs, and sought to satisfy
them. The pre-dynastic Egyptians had begun
to use malachite for face-painting, which neces-
sitated expeditions to Sinai, where copper ore
was to be got ; they needed cowries and gold,
hence the opening-up of Nubia ; they desired
ivory, and evidently went to the Sudan to get
it. Similarly the needs of the Cretans led them
afield to open up fresh countries. In this way
these early people set in motion a process
that was destined eventually to cover the earth,

and to lead to the foundation of civilizations in many countries. The early civilization of the Ancient East was spread over a compact area, for feminine figurines are found fairly evenly distributed from Italy to Mesopotamia.

This early civilization had certain fairly well-defined limits ; and the manner of its growth suggests the ordinary expansion of a civilization that is constantly elaborating fresh needs and seeking to satisfy them, or is discovering in outlying places fresh sources of raw materials for their industries, and thus is opening up the neighbouring countries. The settlement in Sumer, for instance, seems to have been that of people, well versed in the craft of irrigation, who thought the place well suited for occupation, and set to work to drain the marshes and dig irrigation canals. And other settlements seem to have had some such homely origin.

But something happened that sent a wave of culture from one end of the world to the other. Men, for some reason or other, suddenly began to move through great distances, and to implant, in widely separated spots, a distinctive civilization, the like of which men had not seen before, and have not seen since. There are no signs of a gradually and continuous development in the widely scattered regions where this civilization was implanted ; rather are the signs those of a more or less sudden dispersal of culture. This new phase of civilization was characterized especially by the building of monuments of large stones. The megalith builders appeared in Britain, France, Spain and Portugal, Denmark and Sweden, North Germany, and in a few other places in Europe ; in Syria ; in North Africa ; in the Caucasus ; in Siberia ; in Korea ; in India ; and in a far-flung line of settlements reaching from India to America (2). The typical megalithic monuments are dolmens, stone circles, standing stones and pyramids, with their derivative types. These monuments are, it appears, not found in any numbers in the area of the first civilization, but begin on its outskirts and extend to the ends of the earth.

This civilization of megalith builders that is found in all parts of the world was characterized by other cultured elements. The people usually practised irrigation or terraced cultivation ; they made polished stone implements ; they carved stone ; they worked metals. It is well known that the first food-producing people who arrived in western Europe, including this country, were small, brown-skinned, long-skulled men, who brought with them the practice of growing cereals, evidently on the terraces that they made on the hill-sides of England, Wales and other countries of western Europe ; these terraces, in southern France and northern Spain, presumably being irrigated. These men came up from the Mediterranean, and there is every reason to believe that their culture was derived, directly or indirectly, from Egypt of the Pyramid Age. From the fact that the communities that built megalithic monuments practised irrigation the world over, it is probable that they were derived, directly or indirectly, from Egypt. This probability becomes much greater when the stone monuments that they erected are considered. The most interesting megalithic monument is the dolmen, and much discussion has been expended on its origin. The problem has, however, finally been solved by Elliot Smith, who has shown that it is nothing more or less than a degenerate Egyptian mastaba tomb, the type of tomb made by the ruling class in the early dynasties (3). That being so, the world-wide spread of civilization must, for yet another reason, be regarded as originating in Egypt. Again, the making of polished stone implements must probably be ascribed to the Egyptians, who, while working the gold mines of Nubia, used the local forms of stone for implements, instead of the flint that they invariably used in the valley of the Nile itself.

Since the Egyptians were sending out expeditions to Punt, Sinai and Syria, led by nobles or men of royal blood, it is probable that they sent others to Spain and Portugal and other countries of western Europe. The Egyptians, it must be remembered, were the originators of ships, of that there can be no doubt; so that all maritime activity must, especially in its initial phases, have been influenced profoundly by them. Knowing, as we do, the keenness of the Egyptian search for raw materials, the presence of dolmens in the regions of Spain, Portugal, France and other countries that provide gold, copper and other materials, need cause no surprise : it is the natural consequence of the activities of this people.

It can be shown, the world over, that the settlements of megalith builders were, so far as is known at present, invariably situated near sources of valued substances, often those desired as givers of life.   The early wanderers evidently were attracted by the stores of gold, copper, lead, and so forth that this country and Ireland contained, for the distribution of the dolmens and other monuments coincides with the sources of these materials.   We know, too, that these materials were being used by the peoples of the Ancient East in times when the stone mastaba, the prototype of the dolmen, was in constant use.   The dolmens of North Africa, Armenia and the Caucasus are near sources of materials such as gold, copper and iron. The dolmen builders of India lived in the proximity of gold, copper, iron and diamond workings, the gold mines revealing a great command of the technique of mining.   The dolmens of Korea are near some of the richest gold mines of the world.   The ancestors of the Polynesians, who can be traced from India right out across the Pacific, invariably left their remains, dolmens, pyramids and stone circles near sources of pearls, and sometimes of gold. In America, again, the oldest civilizations, those of Guatemala and Mexico, of Colombia and of Peru, were situated near sources of gold and other minerals.   The mound-builders of the

United States, who left dolmen burial chambers in some of their mounds, were settled in the regions richest in gold and pearls, both of which things they regarded as life-giving.

Not only have the builders of megaliths chosen for settlement those countries which contained supplies of givers of life, but there is likewise good reason for concluding that the first food-producing people in Central Asia were attracted thither by its stores of gold. They were irrigators, and the ruins of their irrigation systems are to be found along the banks of the rivers whose gravels contained gold: those rivers barren of gold are devoid of irrigation systems. It is known, also, that these irrigators used gold. So there is reason for believing that the distribution of this precious substance mainly determined their settlements. The Chinese cannot explain why jade and gold are identified with the source of life. They apparently did not elaborate the idea themselves, and their past history goes to show that they must have brought it with them. The first place where Chinese civilization can be detected is in the valley of the Wei, a tributary of the Hoang Ho or Yellow River. Their capital in early times was Siang-fu, on the banks of the Wei, situated, we are told by Laufer, near to important gold and jade mines. This makes it possible to suggest that the bearers of civilization to China came there in search of gold and other precious substances. Who these men were, it is impossible at present to say, but they left behind them, at Siang-fu, some immense pyramids, a form of building unknown to the Chinese (4). The Chinese looked back to the Kwen-lun mountains as the place where lived the immortal Queen of the West, who possessed the magic peach-tree, and these mountains have long been a most important source of jade, as well as containing much gold. This affords a natural explanation of the importance attached by the Chinese to jade and gold.

If the Egyptian origin of the dolmen, as suggested by Elliot Smith, of pyramids, of the practice of irrigation, and of the making of polished stone implements, as well as of ship-building, be accepted, then the spread of early civilization throughout the world is the direct result of Egyptian influence, working directly or indirectly in any particular case. Why, it may be asked, should a great wave of culture suddenly spread out from this one focus in all directions ? Why should Egypt rather than countries such as Crete or Sumer, have this distinction of civilizing the world ? It seems hard to resist the conclusion that the elaboration of ideas of immortality connected with mummification, and therefore with givers of life, was the prime cause of this great movement. As has been pointed out, the ritual rebirth of the dead, which was the central feature of the ritual of mummification, consisted mainly of the utilization of various givers of life. Once it is thought that immortal life is to be got on this earth, there is no limit to the efforts that men will put forth to get it. All ideas connected with givers of life will be immensely strengthened, and men will eagerly ransack the world for such substances. In this way it is possible to account for the apparently haphazard distribution of early civilization throughout the world, and for its great similarities in all places. Moreover, it is possible in this way to account for the preponderating influence of the Egyptians on the civilization of the world. For they had an incentive that was lacking to the people of Sumer, and, presumably, of Crete and other countries where mummification was not practised.

In the earliest literature known to us there are traces of the idea of an earthly paradise, where immortal life was to be had (5). The Sumerians had an idea of an earthly paradise, connected with the mystical land of Dilmun, which is supposed to have been situated on an island in the Persian Gulf, from which gulf came Enki, or Ea, the founder of their civilization. There dwelt Tagtug, the gardener, or Ziusiddu, the survivor of the flood, endowed with immortality, which was denied to men in Sumer. Some human beings could get to this island. In the Babylonian epic of Gilgamesh, the hero visited his ancestor on this island. The name of the ancestor was Uitnapishtim, the Babylonian translation of Ziusiddu, and Gilgamesh was one of his descendants. Gilgamesh incurred the wrath of the goddess

Ishtar, who inflicted a foul disease on him. His companion, Eabani, was in the underworld, and he, resolving, if possible, to escape this fate, determined to go to his ancestor, Uitnapishtim, to get the herb of immortality that he possessed. Uitnapishtim had attained to " the longed-for life in the assembly of the gods," and had the power to " interpret life or death." Gilgamesh went by Mt. Mashu, guarded by scorpion men, and at last reached an enchanted garden in which there was a divine tree : " Precious stones it bears as fruit—the branches were hung with them, lapis lazuli it bears, choice (?) to look upon." When he got to the shore, which is supposed to be that of the Persian Gulf, he met a divine mermaid, whom he persuaded to allow him to cross the sea to the Isles of the Blest, where dwelt Uitnapishtim. He reached them, and Uitnapishtim promised to make him immortal, cured him of his illness, and sent him back with a magic plant, of which we are told that " whoever ate of it regained the strength of his youth." On his way back the plant was snatched from him by the serpent called " Earth Lion," so he lost the chance of immortality.

The reader knows that the Sumerians, and the Babylonians after them, were not able to acquire immortality for themselves. At the same time, the remarks just made show that they were well aware of the fact that certain men could gain this boon. Since the Sumerians played no part in the elaboration of the idea of immortality, it cannot be in Sumer that the raw material out of which was fashioned the story of the earthly paradise, the land of immortal life, can be sought. It is surely in Egypt, the homeland of these ideas, that search must be made.

With the idea of immortality as the privilege reserved for those who had been mummified, there was associated, in Egypt, a belief that the dead so buried lived in the Isles of the Blest, in the company of Osiris. This elysium was situated in a land like the Delta of the Nile, where the happy ones lived in the islands formed by the canals, in a land teeming with wild-fowl, where the crops grew enormously without any cultivation. All was peace and joy. This was the first " Earthly Paradise," a homely place, containing the Tree of Life, which served to reanimate its inhabitants. The Egyptians were, however, interested in another wonderful land, the land of Punt, the God's Land, situated somewhere in Southern Arabia and Somaliland. From at least as early as the beginning of the First Dynasty they were sending expeditions to this marvellous land to get stores of life-giving and other substances that they needed in their temple and funerary ritual, stores of gold, ivory, aromatic gums and resins for incense, feathers, and so forth.

There is some reason to believe that this search on the part of the Egyptians gave rise to the Sumerian civilization. Sumerian records go back to places, Dilmun, Magan and Meluhha, over the seas and reached by ships ; of which places Dilmun was the earthly paradise, and was possessed of stores of copper, while Magan had stores of diorite and copper, and Meluhha was a land of gold. Dilmun was probably in the Persian Gulf ; Magan was, in Babylonian times, identified with Egypt, and Meluhha with Punt, but it is uncertain whether this identification is true in the earliest texts. In any case, it seems certain that the Sumerians were in communication, whether direct or indirect, with Egypt and Punt, which well accounts for their belief in the existence of countries where immortal life is to be got (6).

The contrast between Egyptian and Babylonian ideas is interesting. Egyptians could get to the Isles of the Blest by means of mummification. The Sumerians, who did not practise mummification, could not get there, although they knew of such places. The land of Punt was a real land. for the Egyptians. But the Sumerians, who evidently amalgamated the ideas of Punt and of the Osirian Isles of the Blest, naturally could not get to a land that had no real existence, and was only, in Egypt, accessible to the dead. In Babylonia, in later times, only certain semi-divine beings, akin to the Children of the Sun, could get to the earthly paradise ; other men were forbidden the place. The Babylonian idea of the earthly paradise was complicated : it was mixed up with ideas concerning precious stones. Evi-

dently, in Babylonia, the two sacred lands of
the Egyptians had become fused, the idea
now being that there exists a wonderful land
where immortality is to be had, which is reserved
for the privileged few. That the Babylonians
had identified the land of the dead with places
producing magical substances is further shown
by the account of Sargon of Akkad bringing
gold from the mountains of Aralu, " the home
of the dead beyond the Ocean Stream in the
distant north."

The Hebrew sacred writings contain versions
of the Sumerian and Babylonian stories of an
earthly paradise. The paradise of Genesis
is similar to that of the Babylonians, in that
it is a land, probably irrigated, that possessed
gold and precious stones and a tree of life, a
land with givers of life. The paradise of
Ezekiel, where lived the king of Tyre, was likewise a land with givers of life, among them the
cedar tree, so greatly desired by the Egyptians,
Sumerians and Babylonians, and used by them
in their ritual.

These stories show that the earthly paradise
was regarded as a place where givers of life
were to be had in abundance, and emphasis
is laid, in Babylonia and among the Israelites,
on the presence of gold and other precious
substances. It has just been remarked that
the dolmen builders throughout the world
have chosen to settle in places where they
found gold, pearls, and so forth. What is the
meaning of this distribution ? Does it mean

that men were deliberately seeking the earthly paradise, that they were looking for sources of givers of life, and settling where they found them ?

The evidence certainly all supports this idea. In the first case, it is entirely fitting to find stone monuments of the dolmen and pyramid type in such places ; for, as has been seen, they were built in Egypt some time after the ideas connected with immortality had been elaborated, so that the first builders of these monuments in outlying places would know of such ideas. But it is possible to go much further than that : it is possible to show that an active search was being made through long ages, in all parts of the earth, for the land of immortal youth.

The Chinese formerly had an active belief in givers of life. In their Tao system, which includes the belief in the Isles of the Blest, much mention is made of various " givers of life," prominent among them being gold, jade and pearls. Jade and gold seem to have been the two most powerful magical substances known to the Chinese. In very early times they were identified with the heavens, the source of all life. It is said, " Heaven is jade, is gold . . . jade and gold naturally endow with vitality all persons who swallow them . . . and they hold at a distance from the dead corruption and decay, thus furthering their return to life." As an example of the lengths that the Chinese went in their endeavours to obtain immortality by means of these, and other, substances, the following may be quoted. Ku Koh Sung, an alchemist of the fourth century B.C., says: " Grease of jade is formed inside the mountains which contain jade. It is always to be found in steep and dangerous spots. The jade-juice, after issuing from these mountains, coagulated into such grease after more than ten thousand years. This grease is fresh and limpid like crystal. If you find it, pulverize it and mix it with the juice of herbs that have no pith, it immediately liquifies; drink one pint of it then, and you will live a thousand years. He who swallows gold will exist as long as gold ; he who swallows jade will exist as long as jade. Those who swallow the real essence of the dark sphere (heavens) will enjoy an everlasting existence ; the real essence of the dark sphere is another name for jade. . . . Bits of jade, swallowed or taken with water, can in both these cases render man immortal." Another extract : " Plant the Yang and grow the Yin ; cultivate and cherish the precious seed. When it springs up, it shows a yellow bud ; the bud produces mercury, and the mercury crystallizes into granules like grains of golden millet. One grain is to be taken at a dose, and the doses repeated for a hundred days, when the body will be transformed and the bones converted into gold. Body and spirit will be endowed with miraculous properties, and their duration will have no end." It is not remarkable that these experiments often ended disastrously, and the drinker of the concoction, instead of attaining immortal life on this earth, departed thence in a great hurry.

A significant summary of some of the effects of the belief in the life-giving properties of various substances has been given by Mr. Martin in his work on *The Lore of Cathay*. He says: "Man's first desire is long life—his second is to be rich. The Taoist commenced with the former, but was not long in finding his way to the latter. As it was possible by physical discipline to lengthen the period of life, he conceived that the process might be carried far enough to result in corporeal immortality, accompanied by a mastery of matter and all its potencies. The success of the process, though, like the quest of the Holy Grail, involving certain moral qualifications, depended mainly on diet and medicine; and in quest of these he ransacked the forest, penetrated the earth, and explored distant seas. The natural longing for immortality was thus made, under the guidance of Taoism, to impart a powerful impulse to the progress of discovery in three departments of science—botany, mineralogy, and geography. Nor did the other great object of pursuit remain far in the rear. A few simple experiments, such as the precipitation of copper from the oil of vitriol by the application of iron, and the blanching of metals by the fumes of mercury, suggested the possibility of transforming the baser metals into gold.

This brought on the stage another, and, if possible, a more energetic, motive for investigation. The bare idea of acquiring untold riches by such easy means inspired with a kind of frenzy minds that were hardly capable of the loftier conception of immortality. It had, moreover, the effect of diverting attention particularly to the study of minerals, the most prolific field for chemical discovery."

The Chinese believed in certain Isles of the Blest, where immortality was to be had. "To the east of the Gulf (i.e. the Gulf of Chi-li)—it is not known how many myriads of li distant —there is an ocean, vast in extent, and, in very truth, bottomless. In its fathomless depths is the so-called 'Abyss of Assembly,' to which the waters from the eight points of the compass, and from the uttermost parts of the earth, and from the streams of the Milky Way all flow. And this they do without causing any appreciable change in the depth of the Abyss.

"Here lie the Five Isles, named Tai Yu, Yuan Chaio, Fang Hu, Ying Chou, and P'eng Lai. In height and round its base each island measures 30,000 li, and the circumference of the plateau on the summit of each is 9,000 li. Each is separated from its neighbours by a distance of 70,000 li. Upon their shores the terraces and pleasure towers are built of unblemished white. Thick groves there are, laden with pearls and gems, and not a flower but gives forth a fragrant perfume, nor a fruit but has delicious flavour. On those who eat thereof is conferred the boon of youth and immortality. The inhabitants are all *hsien* and holy sages, who pass their days in happy companionship which the intervening ocean channels do not interrupt, for they float through the air from island to island in countless numbers.

" Now originally the bases of these Five Islands were not anchored in any spot, and in consequence they always followed the movements of the tides, up and down and to and fro, so that never for a moment were they firmly fixed."

These islands were therefore finally fixed to the backs of five gigantic turtles.

The Chinese, intent, as they were, on the search for the elixir of life, did not allow the belief in these Isles of the Blest to remain untested. They went to find them. Major Yetts, in a fascinating paper on the Chinese Isles of the Blest, published in the *Journal of the Folk-Lore Society* for 1919, has made this quite clear. " In the fourth century B.C. the notion was sufficiently established to lead a feudal prince to make search for the Isles of the Blest." Again he says: " At that time when China had become united under the rule of Shih Huang of the Ch'in dynasty, the Emperor travelled to the sea coast. Then magicians in countless numbers discussed the Three Enchanted Islands. The Emperor feared lest, if he himself embarked upon the sea, he might not succeed in reaching them. So he commissioned some one to make the search, whom he provided with a band of young folks, boys and maidens. Their ship sailed across the mid-ocean. The excuse they gave for failure was the plea of contrary winds, declaring that they had been unable to get to the isles, though they had seen them from afar." Other emperors that succeeded him were likewise obsessed with the desire to find the way to the place where they could obtain immortality by virtue of the magical substances there to be found. It is claimed that colonies were thus formed by the Chinese in the Philippines and in Japan.

The Chinese were not alone in their belief in the Isles of the Blest, nor in their efforts to reach the Earthly Paradise. We find an analogous idea in possession of the Japanese, as is natural for a people who have inherited so much from the Chinese. They call the Isles of the Blest, Horaisan, " the land of everlasting life, where is the mountain of immortality. On it grows a wonderful tree with roots of silver, a trunk of gold, and fruits of rare jewels. The finest flowers and fruits, all unfailing, grow there ; eternal spring reigns ; the air is always sweet, the sky always blue. The place is rarely found by mortals, though many have sought for it, for it is visible only for a moment afar off." Stories are told, however, of men who managed to get to these islands.

The earthly paradise formed part of the beliefs of India, as expressed in the great epics of the *Mahabharata* and the *Ramayana*. These works describe certain lands lying to the

north. The northernmost of all is Uttarakuru,
the place where dwell the Siddhas, men who
by their virtues have attained to immortality.
The multiplicity of rivers that exist there points
to numerous islands on which live the blessed.
It is said to lie in the extreme north, where the
sun and moon cease to shine. Journeying on
northward you come ultimately to the river
Sailoda, whose water petrifies those who touch
it. " On either bank of that river grow reeds
called Kichaka, which carry the blessed
(Siddhas) to the opposite bank, and back.
There is Uttarakuru, the abode of the pious,
watered by lakes with golden lotuses. There
are rivers by thousands, full of leaves of the
colour of sapphire and lapis lazuli, and the
lakes, resplendent like the morning sun, are
adorned with costly jewels and produce precious
stones, with gay beds of lotuses of golden
petals. Instead of sand, round pearls, costly
jewels, and gold form the banks of the rivers,
which are covered with trees of precious stones,
trees of gold shining like fire. The trees
always bear flowers and fruits, they swarm
with birds, they are of a heavenly smell and
touch, and yield all desires ; other trees bring
forth clothes of various shapes. . . . All the
inhabitants do pious deeds, all are given to love,
all dwelling together with their wives, have
their desires fulfilled. There one always hears
the sound of song and music mixed with gay
laughter, pleasant to all creatures. There is
none who does not rejoice, none whose desires

are not fulfilled ; and every day these pleasant
qualities grow brighter."

The belief in an earthly paradise was
possessed by the Greeks, and, following them,
the Celts. Hesiod speaks of it. The Greeks
believed in a happy land in the north, inhabited
by people called the Hyperboreans, which
has been located by some in the Baltic. The
settlement of dolmen-builders is interesting
in this connection. For the distribution of
the remains of this early civilization coincides
exactly with that of amber. This substance
was highly prized by the people of the Mediterranean for thousands of years, and it is
mentioned by Homer as worn in jewellery.
It therefore would seem that some deep-seated
relationship existed between the amber and
the idea of the Hyperboreans.

The Celts, who owed much to Greek civilization, had well-developed ideas of the earthly
paradise, and they, too, went out to seek it.
In *The Voyage of Bran*, translated by Professor
Kuno Meyer, with Mr. Alfred Nutt as com-
mentator, there is an account of mysterious
isles visited by the hero. A mysterious woman
comes one day to Bran, son of Febal, " when
the royal house was full of kings," and described
to him the Isles of the Blest. She bare him
a branch of apple-blossom.

> " A branch of the apple-tree from Emain
> I bring, like those one know ;
> Twigs of white silver are on it,
> Crystal boughs with blossoms.

" There is a distant isle,
    Around which sea-horses glisten ;
    A fair course against the white-swelling surge,
    Four feet uphold it.

.   .   .   .

" Unknown is wailing or treachery
    In the familiar cultivated land.
    There is nothing rough or harsh,
    But sweet music striking the ear.

.   .   .   .

" Wealth, treasure of every hue,
    Are in Cuin, a beauty of freshness,
    Listening to sweet music,
    Drinking the best of wine."

There are thrice fifty of the isles, lying distant to the west of Ireland. Bran and his followers set out thither, and arrived at the Isle of Joy, where one of them was left behind. Then they reached the Isle of Women, the queen of which draws Bran's boat to shore. The wanderers stay there until longing seizes them to go home. They find on arrival there that they have been absent for centuries. Bran, after telling of his adventures, disappears from mortal ken.

The story of the voyage of Bran does not stand alone in Celtic literature. As Mr. Nutt says : " The voyage of Saint Brendan, which touched so profoundly the imagination of mediæval man, which was translated into every European tongue, which drove forth adventurers into the Western Sea, and was one of the contributory causes of the discovery of the New World,—the voyage of Saint

Brendan is but the latest and definitely Christian example of a genre of story-telling which had already flourished for centuries in Ireland, when it seemed good to an unknown writer to dress the old half-pagan marvels in orthodox monkish garb, and thus start them afresh on their triumphal march through the literature of the world."

If, as Mr. Nutt says, the story of the Isles of the Blest led many a wanderer out to seek his fortune, and played a part in the events leading to the discovery of America, it is but fitting to find that the people of Mexico believed that the bringers of civilization to their country came seeking for the earthly paradise. "In coming southward (into Mexico) to seek the earthly paradise," the historian says, "these men certainly did not deceive themselves, for it is the opinion of those who know that it is under the equinoctial line: and in thinking that it ought to be a high mountain they are also not mistaken, for, so say the writers, the earthly paradise is under the equinoctial line, and it is a very high mountain, whose summit almost touches the moon. It appears that these men or their ancestors had consulted an oracle on this matter, either a god or a demon, or they possessed an ancient tradition that had been handed down." Apparently they found the place, which was named Tollan, and in the subsequent movements of these peoples the name of Tollan was carefully preserved. These strangers who

were seeking the earthly paradise were, so
Torquemada says, great artists, who also worked
gold and silver. They arrived at Tollan, a
land of abundance of wealth, the earthly
paradise. All sorts of food grew there in the
greatest profusion, and cottons of all colours.
There were birds with rich plumage and beauti-
ful melodious voices. There grew the best
cocoa, as well as the black gum that was so
highly prized. It is also, we are told, the place
where are found emeralds, turquoises, gold
and silver. The Mexicans were so steeped
in traditions of this sort, of tales of the arrival,
in the past, of wonderful strangers, that they
greeted Cortez and the Spaniards as beings
of the same order, come once again to bring
them the blessings of civilization. They were
soon disillusioned.

The fact that the founders of civilization
in all parts of the world have chosen certain
places for settlement rather than others,
these places being those with supplies of
givers of life, harmonizes well with the
stories of the earthly paradise, and with the
historical instances of search having being
made for such places. It shows that these
stories recount the usual manner by which
early civilization spread over the earth. The
seekers after the earthly paradise have found
it over and over again. The Celts of Ireland
imagined that there was a land of eternal
youth, full of magical substances, over the
sea. But what was the place where they lived,

Ireland itself, but a region that must in early times have possessed great stores of gold, pearls and purple, which substances were, it would seem, actively exploited by the ancients. The dolmen builders settled in Cornwall, there to work the gold that they found in the rivers. When we find that the castle of King Arthur, the central figure of a cycle of stories concerning the search for givers of life, in this instance in the form of the Holy Grail, was at Tintagel, in the midst of the Cornish mining region, it would seem that, once again, there is some deep-seated connection between the supply of life-giving substances and the stories of the search for them. The founders of the civilization of Mexico had a culture which included the building of megalithic monuments, the making of polished stone implements and the working of metals. They arrived in Mexico seeking the earthly paradise, we are told. They settled there, and thence sent out other expeditions on the same errand. These presumably got to their destination, for traces of Mexican influence are to be found in the parts of the United States that contain supplies of gold, pearls and turquoise, all of them prized as givers of life by the Mexicans. The evidence, therefore, all goes to show that the ancients held concrete ideas with regard to the earthly paradise, the land possessing givers of life. They sought out, in all parts of the earth, places with gold, pearls and so forth, and there established civilization. Each community so established treasured the belief in some distant source of life, and played its part in the process of propagation. This search would inevitably have covered the earth, were it not that, in the course of time, warfare developed in all parts of the world, and men's minds became obsessed with other ideas.

Thus there is every reason to believe that the elaboration, by the Egyptians, of the idea of immortality, and the subsequent development, the details of which are not yet quite clear, of the notion of an earthly paradise, ultimately led to the transplantation of civilization to the uttermost ends of the earth. It stimulated the minds of men to make all manner of researches in the endeavour to obtain this precious gift, and ultimately led to the development of scientific thought. It has left behind it, all over the world, a precipitate of thought and practice that is still active, as will be shown in Chapter VIII. For the early seekers after immortality have taught the native peoples in all parts of the earth to use givers of life for all manner of practical purposes, and have provided them with the technical means of carrying on their magical crafts. They have also provided an inexhaustible theme for romance, as is shown by the many cycles that deal with the search for immortality.

CHAPTER V

THE CHILDREN OF THE SUN

ALL has not yet been said about the topic of the earthly paradise. For something can be learned about those who went out to seek it—who also found it—and this knowledge helps still further to emphasize the fact that the movement must be regarded as having originated in Egypt. It is evident, from certain of the stories, such as the Babylonian, Indian, Celtic and Japanese, that only certain favoured mortals could get to the earthly paradise, and partake of its benefits. In the Babylonian Gilgamesh epic, only Gilgamesh could get to the Isles of the Blest: Bran, the son of a king of Ireland, goes with his followers to the Isles of the Blest: in India certain favoured mortals could go to the earthly elysium. How comes it that immortality is only available for the few? What is the historical meaning of this incident? What meaning are we to attach, for instance, to the statements in Ezekiel, where the king of Tyre, who is described as a "god," is said to live in paradise? "Moreover, the word of the Lord

came unto me, saying, Son of man, take up a
lamentation for the king of Tyre, and say unto
him, Thus saith the Lord God : Thou sealest
up the sum, full of wisdom, and perfect in
beauty.   Thou wast in Eden in the garden of
God ; every precious stone was thy covering,
the sardius, the topaz, and the diamond, the
beryl, the onyx, and the jasper, the sapphire,
the emerald, and the carbuncle, and gold . . .
and I set thee, so that thou wast upon the
holy mountain of God. . . ."   (Ezek. xxviii. 11
et. seq.).

If reference be made back to Egypt, where
the ideas of immortality and of the earthly
paradise appear to have originated, it is found
that, in the beginning, only members of the
royal family were entitled to such benefits.
Mummification was the means to immortality.
The earthly paradise was therefore an exclusive
place.   In his *Works and Days*, Hesiod says
that the Isles of the Blest are only for semi-
divine heroes, the sons of the gods.   The earthly
paradise, therefore, seems to have been a close
preserve for men who claimed divine birth.
Since the only place where any signs exist of
the origin of the idea of divine descent is Egypt,
where the Children of the Sun were the first
men to call themselves sons of gods, it would
be expected that the Greek heroes, who alone
had access to the Isles of the Blest, were, therefore, connected with the Children of the Sun,
that they belonged to this family.   These
Children of the Sun were, in Egypt, closely

associated with the idea of immortality—for it is in the Pyramid Texts that such ideas are most vividly expressed—so they are suitable men to be able to go to the place where immortality is to be found. Can we, therefore, discover traces of the Children of the Sun in places where givers of life exist, places with traces of a former occupancy on the part of men who had a high degree of civilization ? Can we parallel, in other parts of the earth, the description of the king of Tyre, a god living in Paradise, and associated with all manner of givers of life ? In fact, was the great spread of civilization led out from Egypt by the Children of the Sun ?

In Europe, there is little evidence to reveal the identity of the builders of the long barrows, dolmens and other megalithic monuments, except that they presumably had leaders of high rank. This phase of development seems to have been one of exploitation, pure and simple, not of colonization, and for the present purpose it can be left on one side. The phase of European culture called the Bronze Age, on the contrary, reveals probable signs of the Children of the Sun. At some time in the past, which is reckoned at the beginning of the Middle Minoan period in Crete (about 2200 B.C.), and progressively later as we go westwards, there appeared in Europe, beginning with Crete and the eastern Mediterranean, a new type of grave, consisting of a bee-hive chamber with a corbel roof, made of dry stone

walling, and not of large slabs, as in the case
of dolmens, and approached by a long gallery
of dry stone walling, the whole covered by a
great mound of earth or rubble. Graves of
this type exist at Maes Howe in the Orkneys,
and New Grange in Ireland. This new phase
of culture is characterized also by the use of
solar symbols, which previously had been
absent in Europe; also by small triangular
daggers of copper or bronze; also by the pro-
fuse use of gold ornaments. These graves
show strong signs of Egyptian influence: in
the first place they are modelled, so we are
told by Professor Flinders Petrie, on the
pyramids of the Twelfth Dynasty in Egypt;
in the case of Crete and elsewhere in the
Eastern Mediterranean, the graves of this type
contain models of mummies, or else embalmed
bodies. Sir Arthur Evans claims, in his work
on *Mycenœan Tree and Pillar Cult*, that the
Cretans derived their solar symbolism from
Egypt. Therefore a continuity runs right
through from Egypt to the furthermost bounds
of Europe in respect of this movement of culture.

The interpretation of these facts is, of course,
only conjectural; but the conclusion that
accords best with the whole of the facts derived
from a world-wide study of the sun-cult, and
of the movement of culture in general, is that
this new influence marks the setting-out, from
Egypt, of members of the royal family of the
Children of the Sun, who came to power at the
beginning of the Fifth Dynasty. The dagger

is a sign of noble or royal birth in early Egyptian
hieroglyphs, so the use of the dagger points
to noble or royal birth ; the great tombs suggest
men of great importance ; so does the lavish
use of gold for ornaments ; and the solar
symbols suggest the sun-cult, that is so inextricably bound up with the Children of the Sun
from one end of the earth to the other. It
is well known that the Children of the Sun
lived in Europe, for Greek and Celtic mythologies contain many references to them. These
men of divine birth were remembered in later
times as heroes. Not only were they of divine
birth, and privileged to go to the earthly
paradise, but they seem also to have sought
the place in the same practical manner as the
Chinese Emperors. This is suggested by the
story of Heracles and his companions—who
were beings of the same order as the Children
of the Sun, in that they were children of gods—
who went out to seek the Golden Fleece. They
arrived at Colchis, a land famed in antiquity
for its gold, though but little trace of it now
exists, a land, moreover, said, by Herodotus,
to have been colonized by the Egyptians. In
view of what has gone before, what is this story
but that of the eternal quest, a story of the
arrival of heroes in a " paradise," which they
found already tenanted by a " god," by a Son
of the Sun ?

The story of the Argonauts has a wider bearing. For Heracles, one of them, was closely
connected with the Phœnicians, with Melcarth,

the god of Tyre, the king of which, a " god " himself, lived in Eden, in possession of innumerable givers of life. That a man so closely connected with the Phœnicians as Heracles should act as he did, is but in keeping with the characteristics of the rulers of the Phœnicians.

The story of St. Brendan of Ireland, already mentioned in this book as a monkish version of the story of Bran's voyage to the Isles of the Blest, contains valuable evidence that goes far to identify the original hero with the Children of the Sun, for St. Brendan was born of a theogamy. It says, in the Rev. C. Plummer's translation of the *Lives of the Irish Saints*, that: " In the time of Oengus, son of Natfraech, king of Munster, was St. Brendan born. He was of Cairraighe Luachra ; that is, to speak precisely, his noble, well-born, devout and faithful father, Findlug, belonged to Alltraighe Caille. And this couple (i.e. F. and his wife) lived in discipline and lawful wedlock under the rule of Bishop Erc. Now the mother of Brendan saw a vision before he was born. (It seemed to her that) her bosom was full of pure gold, and that her paps shone like snow. When she told this to Bishop Erc, he said that a wondrous birth would be born to her, who would be full of the grace of the Holy Ghost, meaning Brendan " (pp. 44–5). His manner of birth was therefore like that of the Children of the Sun in Egypt. (See p. 41.)

There is thus a certain amount of evidence that the seekers for the earthly paradise in

Europe belonged to the family of the Children of the Sun. But the evidence is far clearer in the outlying parts of the world. Although it is not possible to view the process clearly in the basin of the Mediterranean, and reliance has to be placed mainly on inference, it is otherwise in the region stretching from India, by way of the East Indian Archipelago, and Oceania, to America. Throughout that vast region it can be shown that the rulers of the first food-producing communities, those that built megalithic monuments and had the other cultural characteristics already described, were the Children of the Sun. The evidence varies, but as we travel eastward it gains in clarity. It is vague in India, for that country, like the Ancient East, has been much tormented by invasions, so that the past is largely obliterated : nevertheless, the earlier known ruling families were Children of the Sun. In Indonesia it can be shown that the Children of the Sun settled near sources of gold, pearls, copper and so forth, in Java, Timor, Celebes, Halmahera, the Moluccas and elsewhere. This is true likewise of the Pacific, where the Children of the Sun can be traced from one end to the other, always in the vicinity of the pearls that they so desired. In America the rulers of the early civilizations of Mexico, Colombia and Peru were likewise the Children of the Sun. In Japan the Mikado is the direct descendant of the sun-goddess Amateras. Thus this family has provided rulers for all parts of the world, and one branch, the Japanese, still maintains its power.

The process of civilizing the remote countries of the world seems therefore to have been continuous. A civilization was planted in one country : it then sent out a shoot to another ; and this went on until the greater part of the world was covered with communities ruled over by the same great family, who had sent out members to rule over the various communities that were being formed in places with givers of life. The *Mahabharata* mentions several instances of members of the solar race setting out to seek fresh kingdoms and never returning. On the other hand, it will be remembered that the American people tell of the coming of the Children of the Sun seeking the earthly paradise. We therefore have knowledge of the process from both ends. Since this process apparently was continuous, since the ruling group of one community sent out, as in India, members to rule over another community, it should follow that the culture of these early civilizations should be similar, and that ample signs should be evident of the culture of their original homeland, that is, Egypt. As I have shown in *The Children of the Sun*, the cultures of communities ruled over by the Children of the Sun are strikingly similar to that of Egypt in the Pyramid Age, that is, from the Third to the Sixth Dynasties.

Prior to the Fifth Dynasty, the civilization of Egypt was gradually developing, and new ideas and practices were constantly coming into being. The unification of the country under one king, the work of the founder of the First Dynasty, made a permanent impression on the organization of the State. The king was master of Upper and of Lower Egypt, and was protected by the vulture of the south and the uræus (the asp) of the north; his crown was double, and was an arrangement of the red and white diadems, red for Lower Egypt, white for Upper Egypt; his palace was the " double great house "; the treasury was double, so were the granaries. This duality ran right through the administration of the State, and it was never forgotten that Egypt was dual. In addition, as the result of the coming to power of the Children of the Sun at the beginning of the Fifth Dynasty, the ruling power was split into two, the king performing the sacred offices, while members of another family, usually of Memphis, or of Abydos, acted as viziers. In the Sixth Dynasty the royal family seems to have intermarried systematically with that of the vizier. The kings of these days were buried in pyramids, and went to the sky at death : the nobles were buried in the old mastaba tombs, and went to the Osirian land of the dead, which, in the later dynasties at least, was underground. Both royalty and nobles were mummified, while the commoners were buried, like the pre-dynastic Egyptians, in shallow graves in the sand.

Such were, in broad outlines, the conditions in Egypt at the time of the Sixth Dynasty. This is the type of civilization that appears, in conjunction with the Children of the Sun, in outlying parts of the world, in places with supplies of gold, pearls, and so forth. Although the first links of the chain are missing, yet enough is known of the later times, the evidence of continuity is so strong, that it is possible to urge that the process began, in Egypt, with the expeditions to Punt, which were always led by men of noble, if not of royal, birth. Since continuity exists from Ceylon to America, it is not asking too much to urge that the expeditions to Punt led, in time, to others to India, which established the civilization of the Malabar coast and of the Indus valley, which latter place was an important starting-place for the solar race in India, and this set the process in action. In this way it is possible to explain the existence of a line of settlements, with pyramids, mummification of rulers, sun-cult, dual organization, sacred and war chiefs, whose families intermarried, extending in a long line from India to America. The civilization of these communities is so uniform that I have termed it the *Archaic Civilization*.

It will help to the better appreciation of this process if it be mentioned that the Phœnicians themselves resemble the communities of the archaic civilization of Polynesia and elsewhere so closely that they can be equated to them.

They had the dual organization, much metal-working, the building of megalithic monuments, mummification of rulers, and so forth. They originated, so they say, in the Bahrein Islands in the Persian Gulf, the seat of important pearl fisheries ; and, according to Elliot Smith, they resembled the Polynesians in physical type. Their activities can readily be appreciated from a perusal of the twenty-seventh chapter of Ezekiel. Since their divine rulers lived in Eden, since they were also seeking incessantly after givers of life, they constitute a type of the communities that were originated by the Egyptians when they went out to seek countries with stores of givers of life.

Before setting out, in the chapters that are to follow, to describe the part played by this great transplantation of civilization in building up the religious systems of the world, it is necessary to outline briefly the subsequent fate of this group of early civilizations that were founded in India, America and elsewhere. The settlements of the archaic civilization were not destined to persist. In time the old order broke up, and gave rise to many communities, all of them lower in culture than the original communities. This was due to the fact that the archaic civilization rested on an insecure basis, as may well be understood from its mode of formation in Egypt. When the Children of the Sun got into power, they had to reckon with the old ruling group, and eventually, it seems, they amalgamated with them ;

the result being that, at the end of the Sixth Dynasty, the territorial nobles, who had secured themselves in power at the beginning of the Fifth Dynasty, finally managed to overturn the ruling power, and produced chaos in the country. Precisely the same thing happened throughout the area of the archaic civilization ; the nobles finally killed or banished the Children of the Sun, and we hear no more of them. This ushered in a new epoch of the world's history, that of warrior aristocracies.

The archaic civilization also gave rise to other communities of a lower order, as the result of migration. Thus, for instance, the first civilization of the northern half of America was that of the Maya of Guatemala and Yucatan. The Maya civilization gave rise to others in the surrounding countries, especially in Mexico, that were not quite so advanced as itself in the arts and crafts. The foundation of these early civilizations was maize-growing, which, according to tradition, was discovered by the seekers after the earthly paradise who founded the civilization. These new civilizations in time gave rise to others. For instance, that of Mexico sent out processes to New Mexico and Arizona, and into the eastern States, in order to exploit the turquoise, gold, pearls, and copper that they contained. These civilizations were also founded on maize-growing, which was the universal mode in the South. As time went on these new civilizations gave rise to fresh communities, still similar to them in culture, but on a lower level in the arts and crafts. Each settlement lost something of the original culture, so that the series of civilizations that emerged from the original civilization of the Maya formed a descending scale of culture. The final stage of this process was the work of the Spaniards. They introduced the horse; and the Indians of the eastern States, finding horse-riding an excellent aid to catching buffalo, went out across the Mississippi after these animals, and abandoned much of their former civilization, becoming almost entirely hunters, and not even thinking of domesticating the buffalo. The remarkable feature of this great process is that there is no trace whatever, throughout the whole region of North America, of the invention of a single important element of culture subsequent to the Maya civilization, which, therefore, must have been the work of strangers.

This process of filiation of culture is not peculiar to America : it is characteristic of all parts of the earth, with the exception of the Ancient East. Everywhere it is found that the earliest food-producing communities, those of the archaic civilization, were more advanced in culture than their successors, and that the later communities derived their culture from their predecessors. The superiority of the earlier peoples can easily be seen in the southern part of Africa, where the great ruins of Zimbabwe, and other places in southern Rhodesia, testify to the presence of highly

civilized men from Arabia, who were engaged
in working the gold and other minerals of the
country long before the present Bantu inhabitants came on the scene (1). Likewise, many
megalithic monuments show that the first
food-producing peoples of the western Sudan
in Africa were on a higher plane of culture
than the negro races now living there. All
the world over it can be shown that the originators of the cultures of existing peoples were
the communities of the archaic civilization
ruled over by the Children of the Sun. The
great Polynesian group of peoples trace back
their origins to India. As their historical
records are examined, each set of traditions
leads back in time to the Children of the Sun,
whether in Tahiti, Hawaii, Samoa or India.
From islands ruled over by the Children of
the Sun communities have set out to people
new places, such as the Gilberts. So far as
the Polynesians are concerned, the fount and
source of their ruling group must have been
the solar race of India. The Children of the
Sun of Indonesia likewise originated in India.
As Sir Harry Johnston has well shown, Africa
owes its civilization to Egypt, the home of the
archaic civilization. Europe also owed her
civilization to the same source. The civilization of central Asia likewise rests on Babylonia
or Egypt, and the early rulers of Persia were
also Children of the Sun. In short, the whole
of the available evidence goes to show that all
the great civilizations of the world derived

their cultural capital, directly or indirectly, from the Ancient East; and, further, that every single food-producing community on the earth is derived from some other food-producing community. There is no particle of evidence, from any part of the world outside the Ancient East, that suggests that a fundamental element of culture, such as pottery-making, weaving, metal-working, agriculture, or any such art or craft, has been independently invented. In every case the community has derived the element of culture from some other community.

It is absolutely essential, for the proper understanding of the great process of development of religious systems in all parts of the world, to realize the existence of this great process of filiation of culture. All communities whose history is known derive their culture from some pre-existing community, and ultimately, it would seem, from the archaic civilization ruled over by the Children of the Sun, which civilization has spread over the earth as the result of the desire for givers of life. This is a fundamental principle, the truth of which is becoming increasingly evident as knowledge increases.

The statements just made refer more especially to communities founded by the men of the archaic civilization, and derivatives from these communities. But another group of communities must be considered. The men of the archaic civilization did not find the countries visited by them entirely empty. There was

52498

often a native population in the food-gathering stage of culture. In some places, such as Guatemala, the strangers settled and founded great civilizations, the native population becoming their subjects. On the other hand, the men of the archaic civilization sometimes only made temporary settlements, and then, for some reason, vanished. But they have been remembered by the natives in their traditions, and all culture is ascribed to their teaching, whence they are called *culture-heroes*. A study of the tales about these beings shows them to be connected intimately with the archaic civilization. For instance, the Indians of the United States have a widespread tale to the effect that they owe their civilization to Twins, often said to be the Children of the Sun. They are said to have taught the ancestors of the tribe the useful arts; to have given them maize and other food plants; to have initiated them into the mysteries of their religious rites; to have framed their laws; and then, having started them on the road to civilization, to have left them. It was thought that culture-heroes such as these would return, and this accounts for the reception given to Cortez. In Central Celebes, among certain communities of the Toradja, everything began with Lasæo, the Sun-Lord, who came among them riding on a white buffalo. He gave them all their laws, rites, arts and crafts. He married one of their women, and his sons became the ancestors of ruling houses in various places

in central Celebes. Lasæo belonged to the
sky-world, so intimately connected, the world
over, with the Children of the Sun, and when
he had done his work he returned there, leaving
his children behind him. The Toradja therefore ascribe their culture to the Children of
the Sun. The culture-heroes of Australia were
also connected with the sky. They are known
under different names, according to the tribes;
but their characteristics are similar, as is the
culture they gave the people. They gave the
Australians their social organization; they
taught them their rites and ceremonies, including circumcision and subincision, for which
purpose they introduced the use of the stone
knife; they taught the native ceremonies to
procure food; they instituted marriage rules;
they even gave the people their weapons; in
short, they gave them all their culture.

If a study be made of tales of culture-heroes
from any part of the world, it soon becomes
evident that these beings were closely connected with the archaic civilization: often
they are demonstrably the Children of the Sun.
The characteristics of these heroes are such
that they could hardly have been invented
independently by the native populations to
account for their culture. The tales told of
these beings bear the imprint of history;
the facts they recount are, in some measure,
substantially true.

It will be found, the world over, that the
culture-heroes were visiting places with ample

stores of givers of life : they were on their eternal quest for immortality. Australia, Central Celebes, Luzon of the Philippines, and other places so visited by them, are full of such things. The fact that they did not always leave their descendants behind them is due, as we know in certain cases, to accidental circumstances which prevented them from making permanent settlement. They knew where the promised land was, but they were not destined to occupy it.

CHAPTER VI

GODS AND MEN

THE spread of civilization was due to the desire for givers of life, that were to be found in the earthly paradise. The earthly paradise was a place with great quantities of gold, pearls, and other desired substances. Access to it was reserved for favoured mortals, for the sons of the gods. All the world over it is found that traces exist of the presence of people with a high degree of civilization in such places, and the cultures of all these communities are so similar to that of Egypt in the Pyramid Age as to afford every reason to believe that they were derived from that source. Since access to the earthly paradise was reserved for sons of the gods, since, also, the idea of divine descent evidently began in Egypt, it would be expected that these early communities in the earthly paradises would be ruled over by the Children of the Sun. Inquiry shows this to be the case. The scheme outlined in the past two chapters is therefore harmonious.

It is now necessary to proceed further, and

to inquire into the nature of the religious
system of the archaic civilization, derived,
as it evidently was, from Egypt, and into
the transformations that it underwent when
the archaic civilization broke up ; when, also,
members of the archaic civilization visited
native tribes and did not settle among them.
We have seen the system grow up ; we will
now see what happened when it was transplanted.

One general principle must be laid down
when studying early religious systems :—
namely, that the political, social and economic
aspects of the life of a community are reflected
in the religious system. The religious system
is not formed in a vacuum, as it were ; it
has grown up with the community and therefore bears every sign of its manner of development. This has been made clear in the case
of the origin of the idea of a god, which evidently
was dependent on the coming into being of
ruling groups. The attributes of gods are
derived from earthly life, from arts and crafts,
from rulers, and not from the imagination.
This intimate connection between all aspects
of the life of a community can readily be
observed in Japan, the rulers of which are
descendants of the great sun-goddess Amateras.
The system of Shinto—the way of the gods—
the national cult of Japan, can only be understood when its relations to Japanese history
are remembered (1). The Mikado is himself the
high priest of the national sun-cult, which is

associated with his ancestress. As high priest he is but attending the altar of his ancestors, whose line presumably goes right back into the family of the Children of the Sun at Heliopolis in Egypt. In a country such as Japan, where the religious system, that of Shinto, goes right back to the origins of the State, without any break in continuity, there is the closest possible correspondence between the dignity of the various gods and that of their descendants on earth. The noble families provide the priesthoods for the various shrines that exist, the gods of which are their ancestors. When a noble family is advanced in rank for any reason, the ancestors in the sky-world are ennobled still further. When a noble family is degraded, so are the ancestors. The world of gods consists of a vast hierarchy, with elaborate court ceremonial, just as the world on earth. The proclamation of a republic in Japan would have disastrous consequences in the land of the gods, and we can well picture the consternation caused by such an event. Japan would be reduced to the condition of China, where the old gods have vanished as the result of the elimination of the ruling group, and the people have simply been left with an ancestor-cult.

When the Heliopolitan priesthood elaborated the sun-cult, and made themselves into the "sons" of the sun-god, they were setting in motion a process that had world-wide consequences. Their descendants, more or less direct, in all parts of the earth, are carrying on, or were carrying on during historical times, the sun-cult, partly as a family cult, partly as a state cult, so that, wherever the sun-cult is found in any part of the world, the Children of the Sun will be found also. There is no trace whatever of a sun-cult originating apart from the Children of the Sun : that is a rule without exception, so far as I am aware. There are signs, it is true, of sun-cults of a sort surviving the Children of the Sun, but, as will be shown later (see p. 137 *et seq.*), a definite reason exists for this.

The fact that the sun-cult can disappear with the Children of the Sun, that it was dependent on them for its persistence, and that this disappearance leaves behind it an ancestor-cult, accords well with what is known of the origin of cults of gods and of ancestors in Egypt. In the first instance these two cults were fused, the dead king, Osiris, being both an ancestor and a god. With the coming of the sun-cult, the king carried on cults of the sun-god and of his father, now become Osiris, as did every man who was mummified. Therefore, in this age, the nobles, who did not carry on a sun-cult, would be occupied with the cults of their dead ancestors. Thus it has happened that the break-up of the archaic civilization, the elimination of the Children of the Sun, has everywhere left a marked ancestor-cult.

The Children of the Sun in Egypt presumably owed their position to the doctrine of theogamy, to the claim to divine parenthood. Throughout the world they took this claim with them. The *Mahabharata*, the great epic of India, is full of instances in which the sun-god, in one of his many forms, becomes the father of heroes. In San Cristoval of the Solomons, where the Children of the Sun still persist, it is believed that a woman can have a child by the Sun. The stories of old Samoa likewise tell of times when the sun caused a woman to have a child. A like belief was held in old Fiji, where a chief shut up his daughter so that the sun should not see her, but in vain. The Yuchi of the Savannah River in the United States to-day believe that dark-skinned members of the tribe are Children of the Sun by virgin girls. The belief in the fatherhood of the Sun was held by the Incas of Peru. They kept their virgin daughters in convents, away from men, under the charge of one of the royal princesses. If one of them was found with child, she was condemned to death. But if she said that the sun was the father of the child, she was released, and the child was included in the royal family. Such stories as these throw light on the tale of Danae, who, although shut up in a tower by her parents, was approached by Zeus, himself originally a sun-god, in the form of a shower of gold, and became by him the mother of Perseus. This story shows that the Greeks were formerly in touch with a civilization in which such a mode of birth was imagined to be possible. So wherever

the Children of the Sun went they retained
the story of their original mode of birth, that
invented by the Heliopolitans of Egypt, one
of the first pieces of fiction for which man
has been responsible. This idea of theogamy
was a trump card in the hands of these early
rulers. It placed them above the rest of
mankind on a pedestal, so that no one could
rival them in sanctity. Thus it happened that
they might not be looked upon, and were very
rarely seen in public by their subjects. From
India to Peru the sight of the face of a Son
of the Sun was supposed to have disastrous
consequences for his subjects.

The Heliopolitan priesthood of Egypt invented
the idea of a world in the sky, where dwelt
the sun-god. Shu and Tefnut, the children
of Re, the sun-god, separated earth and heaven,
and Re was borne up to the sky on the back
of the Divine Cow, one of the forms of the
mother goddess, to prepare a land for his followers. The sky-world was, in Egypt, the
exclusive prerogative of the Children of the
Sun ; so it was throughout the world : it was
believed that the sky-born beings could go to
and fro from the sky ; that they could attend
council meetings in their ancestral home : the
culture-heroes who visited various places came
from the sky, and returned there again when
their work was finished ; and when they left
intercourse between sky and earth was more or
less cut off.

It is obvious that the culture-heroes, who were

said to have come from the sky, really came
from some place where dwelt people connected
with the sky, and not actually from the sky
itself. This shows that native tradition does
not actually represent the real past, and for
this reason it has often been claimed that
such tales are obviously imaginative. But in
this case it is possible to reconcile native tradition with what actually must have happened.
For instance, a legend of Hawaii recounts
the doings of a certain " Eyeball of the Sun,"
who lived near Tahiti in a dwelling called
" The Shining Heavens." He was supposed
to be able to fly from place to place, and
his approach was heralded with thunder and
lightning. Thus he was a divine being. The
name of his house suggests that the story of
people coming from the sky may be interpreted in a rational manner, the sky and the
home of the Eyeball of the Sun really being
identical. In Samoa, again, Tagaloa, the founder
of the first ruling family, one of the family
of the Children of the Sun, is said to have
come from the sky; while his wife, Ui, came
across the sea from a place where the sun-god
lived. Actually Tagaloa came across the sea,
so the two statements really mean the same
thing. Since the houses of the Tagaloa family
were regarded as The Heavens, this discrepancy
may again be more apparent than real.

Accession to the throne among the Children
of the Sun did not rest alone on birth. The
Egyptian kings had to be properly consecrated

to their high office, and in the coronation
ceremony they were invested with the regalia.
The crown and the rest of the regalia were
givers of life that protected the king by their
magical powers. The uræus in front of the
diadem was ready to spit out fire and destruction
on those who dared threaten its royal master.
In like manner, the Mikado of Japan has to
possess the sacred mirror, sword and jewel.
The mirror was given by Amateras to her
grandson, Ninighi, when he came to earth.
" Consider it," she said, " as my august spirit,
and reverence it as if you worshipped in my
presence." The sword was also given by
Amateras to Ninighi. It was that of Szannoo,
her brother, who used it to kill the dragon of
Koshi. The jewel was, doubtless, originally
a necklace, an early form of protective device.
All these regalia are kept closely watched.
There is much evidence, not yet collected
and examined, that goes to show that the idea
that the royal power depended largely on the
possession of regalia was spread across the
world with the archaic civilization. The idea
still persists among the Malay chiefs, and in
South Celebes among the Bugi and Macassar
rulers, in spite of their conversion to a nominal
Mohammedanism. The belief in the protective value of givers of life is too deep-
rooted to allow itself to be ignored : even
incarnate gods need all the protection they can
get.

The communities of the archaic civilization,

ruled over by the Children of the Sun, have
in most cases suffered such internal convulsions
that the past has been largely obliterated.
If a careful study be made of gods such as
Zeus of the Greeks, and Mars of the Romans,
it is found that these gods were formerly sun-
gods. In Egypt the sun-god becomes, in
the later dynasties, Amon-Re, and adopts warlike qualities ; in Assyria the national god
is Asshur, a war-god, who has supplanted
sun-gods of the type of Marduk of Babylon ;
in the Vedas of India the chief god is Indra,
a war-god, who has supplanted a group of solar
gods, among whom are Mitra, Varuna and
Surya ; in these and other countries the sun-
gods give way to war-gods. We naturally
inquire why, from one end of the earth to the
other, sun-gods, the chief gods of the archaic
civilization, should be replaced by war-gods,
and we seek in the history of the communities
of the archaic civilization for an answer. The
sun-cult was a family cult among the Children
of the Sun. The disappearance of the sun-
cult therefore suggests some political convulsions in the communities of the archaic
civilization.

Hesiod speaks of the days when peace reigned
over the earth, of the Golden Age. It has
long been customary to regard this as a pious
fiction, as the result of a tendency to idealize
the past. But there can be no doubt that
the story of Hesiod has a substantial basis
in fact. It can be shown, beyond doubt,

that the earliest civilizations of the earth were far more peaceful than those that followed. In Sumer, for instance, there is but little trace of a warlike habit of mind ; but it is far otherwise with Assyria, whose civilization rested on that of Sumer, for that state was a vast war machine. The early Minoan kingdoms of Crete seem to have been mainly peaceful. The same story can be told of the early Teutonic kingdom of Sweden : the king was a sacred king, who had nothing to do with war, and was far different from the kings of later times who swarmed over Europe leaving death and destruction in their wake. Polynesian history recounts of the old days when peace reigned in the Pacific, when chiefs went for thousands of miles to visit their friends, and to join in ceremonies and festivities. Then came a time when fighting began, and the old genial intercourse ceased, when every chief regarded his fellows with suspicion, and spent his time in protecting his property. A gradual increase in the warlike spirit can be observed in Mexico and Guatemala : the first settlements of the Maya in Guatemala show no trace of fighting. Signs of war only occur in the later settlements on the outskirts of this civilization, and the process of education in warfare culminates in the Aztecs.

The story of warfare is that of the gradual education of ruling groups in cruel modes of behaviour. In the beginning the king was probably sacrificed for the supposed good of the

community. Then he evidently managed to
change that custom, and instead of him was
sacrificed a slave or some other victim. This
gave ruling groups power over their subjects,
and it presumably was partly as the consequence of the exercise of this power that warfare, as we know it, gradually developed.
During the times when the Children of the
Sun ruled in all parts of the earth, warfare
was mainly concerned with the procuring of
victims for human sacrifice. But there came
a time when the nobles, who formed a powerful
class in these communities, acquired so much
power that they killed or exiled their divine
overlord, and began to struggle among themselves for power. The rulers henceforth were
less sacred in character, they were more secular
and warlike. They could hardly hope to be
as sacred as the Children of the Sun, for usually
the old order had been so completely broken
up that the proper ritual for the sanctification
of the sacred king was lost. The result of this
break-up was, therefore, the sudden appearance, in all parts of the earth, of military
aristocracies, led by men of royal blood, such
as Odin and his followers in Scandinavia, the
Dorians and other Greek tribes, the Celts, the
Turko-Tartar tribes, the Tai-Shan of Yunnan,
the later Polynesians, the Aztecs, and many
others. One and all, these warrior aristocracies
show patent signs of having but lately emerged
from the condition of culture of the archaic
civilization. The old civilization was founded

on agriculture, usually based on irrigation;
these military wanderers were cattle breeders.
This is true whether we consider the Arabs, who
migrated out of Yemen after the breaking of
the dam of Mahreb; the Aryans, who migrated
into India about 1000 B.C. or earlier; the
Turko-Tartars, or any other similar tribe
or group of tribes. They had dropped the
agriculture of their ancestors, and simply
retained their cattle-breeding habits. In all
parts of the world another curious fact is to
be observed, that the adoption of a new
mode of life involved the transition from
mother-right to father-right. The exact cause
of this transition cannot yet be stated; but
that it occurred within a short time of the
movement of wandering, pastoral, warlike peoples
from their homes is beyond doubt. We are
told this of the Teutons, of the Arabs, of the
Turko-Tartars, of the later Polynesians, and
of those North American Indian tribes that,
having adopted the use of the horse from the
Spaniards, moved out across the Mississippi
into the plains after the buffalo. This growth
of warlike communities was responsible for the
subjection of women. Prior to that they had
been on an equality with men, and, indeed,
in some matrilineal communities, they can
even be said to have ranked slightly higher.
Evidently once warfare became a serious occupation of the men, women were put to a dis-
advantage, on account of their physical dis-
abilities, and thus the notion of the superiority

of man came into being. This notion is now gradually disappearing.

When study is made of the transition from sun-gods to war-gods it can be shown, in more than one case, that sun-gods have actually changed their character and become war-gods, in conformity with the new conditions of society. In Samoa, the Children of the Sun were known as the Tagaloa family. The traditions recount how they came from the sky and settled in the eastern part of the group, bringing with them their temples, regalia and so forth. For some reason or other, the actual details of which are lacking, the pure line of Children of the Sun became extinct, and the chieftainship was carried on by a branch of the ruling group descended from intermarriages between the royal family and the nobles, a branch connected with the under-world, and not, as were the original Tagaloa family, with the sky. The first descendant of this intermarriage, named Tæotagaloa, deliber-ately changed himself into a war-god, and became the first chief, bearing the title of *Tui*, which really is the title of a war chief in Samoa, Fiji and Tonga. From that time onward all direct communication with the sky-world was shut off, and the sole land of the dead and place of residence of gods was the underworld. This is what would have happened in Egypt if the Children of the Sun, with their home in the sky, had been exterminated by the nobles. All connection with the sky-world would have broken off, and all interest would have been concentrated on the Osirian land of the dead, which finally was underground.

Another important instance of the transformation of a sun-god into a war-god, is that given by the Zuni Indians, who live in New Mexico in the Pueblo region of the United States. Their culture-heroes were the Twin Children of the Sun, born of the action of the sun on a foam cap, who changed themselves into war-gods as the result of the growing warlike character of their people.

Who were these war-gods ? In the beginning the rulers were the actual children of the sun-god, and therefore were semi-divine. In the royal family of the Children of the Sun it was believed that a virgin could become the mother of a child through the direct action of the sun. But in communities with war-gods, this belief is not, so far as I am aware, recorded. Yet the war-god himself was sometimes born of a theogamy. For instance, Huitzilopochtli, the great war-god of the Aztecs, was born in that manner. He was supposed also to have been a great warrior who was deified on account of his prowess. In like manner, Oro, or Rongo, the great war-god of the eastern Pacific, was born of a theogamy, and he was also supposed to have been a man. Odin, again, was said to have been as a man, and the founders of the first Anglo-Saxon kingdoms in this country claimed descent from him. Thus war-gods evidently were

men, who belonged to the ruling group of
the archaic civilization, and were born of
theogamies, just like the Children of the Sun.
These men went out with followers, and founded
fresh kingdoms for themselves. Probably, being out on warlike expeditions, they did not,
like the Teutons, take their women with them,
and thus the pure line of the royal family
would die out, the wanderers would be forced
to marry native women, and the possibility
of a theogamy would vanish. Whatever may
be the explanation, the fact that war-gods,
originally supposed to have been men, were
born of a theogamy, goes to show that they
were part of the archaic civilization, and,
consequently, that the communities with war-
gods were directly derived from the archaic
civilization.

The coming into prominence of war-gods
has, in certain parts of the world, had the
effect of stripping off later accretions to the
fabric of civilization, and of revealing the
underlying structure. In Egypt, when the
Heliopolitans came to the throne, the power
was divided between them and the old regime,
for the office of vizier was held by a member
of a family of Memphis or Abydos. The
old ruling group was connected with the Osirian
land of the dead, which ultimately came to be
underground. When the archaic civilization
spread across the world, this condition of
things went with it, so that the various States
had for their ruling group two families that

intermarried, one connected with the sky, and the other with the underworld, the one supplying the sacred chief, the other supplying the war chief. So, in the early days in Samoa, before the disappearance of the Tagaloa family, the Children of the Sun, members of the Tagaloa family married women connected with the underworld. It so happened that the Tagaloa men married women of their own family, and women of the other family, and according to the tales, the offspring of these unions, half-brothers as they would be, were "sacred" and "war" chiefs. Since descent in those days was matrilineal, the child would follow its mother, and thus the son of the woman of the underworld branch of the ruling group would belong to the underworld. So, in later days in Samoa, when the pure line of the Children of the Sun had vanished, connection was had solely with the underworld. This is characteristic of later times throughout Polynesia. In all cases the gods are now in the underworld, and this shows that the underworld branch of the ruling group has triumphed.

In the days when the archaic civilization began to spread from the Ancient East, the mother goddess was still important ; and throughout the world she played a prominent part in the first civilized communities. She has always been closely connected with agriculture. She was the grain goddess in Sumer and Egypt ; and Corn Mothers, Maize Mothers, and Rice Mothers, formed of stalks of cereals bound up together, have played an important part in harvest ritual throughout the world. The archaic civilization was based on irrigation ; so, wherever these people settled, they established irrigation systems, regardless of the suitability or not of the country. They installed irrigation systems in Java and Assam, where the rainfall is immense ; they installed irrigation systems in Arizona, where there is practically none. They did this simply because they knew of no other method of cultivation. Many communities derived from the archaic civilization practise dry cultivation. This provides the extraordinary sight of communities living within a few miles of one another, in Assam, Celebes, and elsewhere, cultivating their food by entirely different methods, communities nearest in culture to the archaic civilization practising irrigation, and those more remote practising dry cultivation.

The Dravidian peoples of India, among whom the mother goddesses were very important, were mostly irrigators. They practised human sacrifice in connection with their agriculture. In Indonesia the people of the archaic civilization, who brought in irrigation, the use of stone and so forth, appear to have been associated with human sacrifice, for it is found in places ruled over by the Children of the Sun, such as Kupang in Timor, where a girl was annually sacrificed in the Bay of Kupang. The Batta of Sumatra, who have strong cultural and racial affinites with the

Dravidians of India, practise human sacrifice
and cannibalism. In most of Indonesia the
archaic civilization has entirely disappeared.
But continuity can be detected between it
and the civilizations now to be found there.
It can be shown that the human sacrifice of
the archaic civilization has, in this region, as
in Melanesia, been replaced by head-hunting,
a less cruel custom. The chief occasions for
this practice are provided by agriculture and
funerals of chiefs, and raids for heads and
raids in retaliation constitute practically the
whole of the warfare of these peoples. They
practise head-hunting for precisely the same
ends as those for which human sacrifice was
instituted. This is but one instance in which
the customs of civilized men are more cruel
than those of so-called savages. In Oceania
human sacrifice is more especially associated
with the archaic civilization, and tends to
die out in those communities where irrigation
is no longer practised, where, consequently,
the old civilization has broken up. In British
New Guinea it takes the form of cannibalism,
and is there especially associated with the
stone circles that exist in certain places, that
is, with remains of the archaic civilization.
The founders of Samoa came from a place
where there was a sun-cult, and where human
sacrifices were made to the sun. The Children
of the Sun in New Caledonia had human
sacrifices in the shape of cannibalism. In
San Cristoval, another place where the Children

of the Sun live, human sacrifice is practised for agriculture. In other parts of Oceania, it tends to die out except when under the direct influence of the archaic civilization. For instance, it has long been given up in Samoa.

In North America the Aztecs practised human sacrifices on an enormous scale in connection with their agriculture. They even practised cannibalism in connection with agriculture. But, further north, human sacrifice becomes rarer in proportion as the cultural level recedes from that of the Mexicans. The Skidi Pawnee, who approach the Mexicans very nearly in culture, have the custom of human sacrifice, but it is unknown among the other branches of the Pawnee. The Plains Indians have almost universally given up the practice, which was only found, in the United States, among peoples such as the Iroquois, who, from their agriculture, showed closest signs of contact with the southern peoples. Human sacrifice was likewise, throughout the archaic civilization, closely associated with the sun-cult. It is only necessary to remind the reader of the practices of the Aztecs in this respect, who slaughtered thousands of victims on the tops of their pyramid temples during festivals connected with their great sun-god.

Communities in which the mother goddess is still prominent, that is, communities directly derived from the archaic civilization, possess that remarkable form of social organization known as mother-right, in which descent in the social group, inheritance of property, and succession to rank go through women, and not through men. It is entirely fitting that the earliest form of society in which the mother goddess was the chief deity should be organized on this basis. In many places it can be seen that the ruling group trace back their descent to a woman, and not to a man. Thus, for instance, in Minahassa of northern Celebes, the founder of the race was Lumimu'ut, a woman who came over the sea in a ship bearing with her all the gifts of civilization, including food-plants. She married her son To'ar, the Sun-god. The genealogical tables of this people trace descent through women for the first few generations, and then change to descent through men. Not only is the mother goddess connected, throughout the archaic civilization, as in Egypt, with agriculture and human sacrifice; not only is she connected with mother-right; she also betrays other character-istics that evidently were derived from the original home of the archaic civilization. The Mexicans, among whom she is an important figure, went to New Mexico and Arizona to work the supplies of turquoise that these States possess. No turquoise exists in Mexico, but it was plentifully used there. The Pueblo Indians, the descendants of the old turquoise miners, still prize it, and they sometimes call their mother goddess Turquoise Old Woman, just as Hathor in Egypt was the Lady of

Turquoise. In like manner, among the Pueblo Indians she has the titles of The Spider Woman, Salt Old Woman, and many others. In India, again, among the Dravidian peoples, the mother goddess has a multitude of epithets, just as in the civilizations of the Ancient East. She is connected with all manner of precious stones, with gold, and with pearls. In Japan the mother goddess is very important. She is the goddess of food above all things ; she is, after Amateras, who is the sun-goddess and the ancestress of the royal line, the most important deity of Shinto. The mother goddess, therefore, tends, in the communities founded by the Children of the Sun, to acquire many characteristics, just as in her homelands.

The mother goddess became unimportant in those communities that acquired war-gods. If she survived at all, she either changed into a god, or became just a wife of a god, and played no active part in affairs. The emergence of war-gods marks the coming of a new epoch, of the subjection of women, of pastoral life, and so forth, and the disappearance of the mother goddess is not the least significant feature of the new order. Prior to that she had been looked on as the mother of the king, but henceforth he is born of woman in the ordinary course. Since the change to war-gods, which means also the change to father-right, involves the disappearance of the doctrine of theogamy, it would seem that the disappearance of the mother goddess has something to do with the political circumstances of the change.

The history of cults of gods, the knowledge that they are maintained by members of royal families claiming descent from these gods, or by deputies appointed by these descendants, shows that the development of religious systems runs parallel with the development of ruling groups. If a new State god appears in any community, it is certain that a new dynasty has arisen : this can be observed in any country. There is a very good reason for this close association between gods and men, a reason which is already familiar to the reader. The gods are the relatives of the kings, and the cult associated with them partly assumes the character of an ancestor-cult. But the cult of the State gods was something more than that : it was a cult connected with agriculture, and with other aspects of the life of the community. Since the early kings, and their divine ancestors, played so useful a part in the lives of the community, it is natural to ask what the commoners thought of it all, what part they played in the matter, and what things really interested them. Two sources of information are open to us. We can study those peoples who once formed part of the archaic civilization, but have lost their ruling class, such as the Pueblo Indians of North America, or we can consider the peoples who were visited by culture-heroes. In either case we shall be dealing with the residuum left behind by the people of the archaic civilization.

It cannot be too emphatically asserted that the history of the world has hitherto concerned itself too exclusively with the doings of ruling groups. This has produced a wrong impression of the nature and development of civilization. It tends, for instance, to cause students to think that the whole of the community was concerned in the compilation of religious systems, when a little thought will show that the commoners could have played practically no part whatever, once the process had begun. The ruling groups presumably began with special knowledge of calendrical systems, and they preserved this knowledge. To this they added other knowledge, and thus tended to buttress their position; while their subjects, especially the ignorant, who formed the vast majority, went on with their daily lives, happy if they could live in peace. The notion that the whole of a community shares in its religious system is false, and the whole of modern speculation on the development of early religion is vitiated on this account. It can be shown, in every part of the world, that the development of early religious systems has been entirely in the hands of rulers claiming relationship with deities.

The cult of the sun-god in Egypt was the care of the king. He it was who, theoretically at least, had to rise each day at dawn and perform the ritual that enabled his august parent to be reborn. This cult, the product of a long process of thought, and concerned with his father, could not possibly interest the commoners. This is shown by the fact that, when the communities of the archaic civilization lost their Children of the Sun, who carried on the sun-cult, the sun-cult usually disappeared. The commoners did not organize it anew. But since the cult of the sun-god was centred round such things as agriculture, it is not likely that the commoners would let everything go. The chief gift of the archaic civilization to the outlying parts of the earth was agriculture. What is more, these old wanderers took certain food plants with them on their wanderings, and made habitable many places. They provided the islands of the Pacific with the bread-fruit, the banana, the coco-nut, the Malay apple, and many other valuable food-plants. In America they took with them the maize northward from Mexico. And throughout the vast region from Egypt to America an underlying uniformity bears witness to the unity of agricultural ceremonies, and therefore of ideas connected with agriculture. These ideas were certainly spread abroad by the people of the archaic civilization. This has caused the native populations, even when they took no notice whatever of the family cults of the strangers, to pay particular attention to agricultural ceremonies, on the assumption that they were absolutely necessary for the proper maintenance of their food-supply. A good instance of this is to be found among the Pueblo Indians of New Mexico and Arizona in North America. They say that they were led by the Children of the Sun to their habitation from their original home in the underworld, but they now have no Children of the Sun ruling over them. They brought maize with them from the under world, that is, from their home in the south. Having no ruling class of Children of the Sun, they have no direct cult of the sun. Most of their ritual centres round the production of food. " They look to their gods for nourishment and for all things pertaining to their welfare in this world, and while the woof of their religion is coloured with poetic conceptions, when the fabric is separated thread by thread we find the web composed of a few simple, practical concepts. Their highest conception of happiness is physical nourishment and enjoyment, and the worship of their pantheon of gods is designed to this end." The ritual of the cults connected with food is identical with that of the ancient Mexicans, and must obviously have been derived thence. When the religious system of the Pueblo Indians, who have no ruling group, is compared with that of the Japanese, who are still ruled over by the Children of the Sun, it is patent what has happened to the religious system of the Indians. The stripping away of the ruling group has caused the disappearance of cults directed towards deities that are ancestors,

and has caused the underlying rites connected
with agriculture, already, as can be seen from
an examination of the Shinto system of Japan,
of great importance, to come into the fore-
ground.

The great powers of persistence of ideas
connected with agriculture are revealed by
the collections of facts made by Sir James
Frazer in his work on *Spirits of the Corn and
the Wild,* where, following Mannhardt and
others, he shows how that the agricultural
peoples of Europe still practise rites that
must go back to the beginnings of civilization.
When the corn grain became equated to the
Great Mother, on account of its resemblance
to the cowrie shell, when trees became equated
to the Great Mother because their sap was
regarded as milk, there was set in motion
a process of practice that only the advance
of real knowledge was able to arrest. This
system of belief constituted the first attempt
at a scientific explanation of the facts of nature
as they affected men in their procuring of
food, and this system only gave way to another
based on facts.

Although the mother goddess goes into
the background in those communities in which
the part of the ruling class connected with
the underworld has gained power and changed
the sun-god into a war-god, or supplanted
him by a war-god, yet in communities such
as those of the Pueblo Indians, which have
had direct contact with the Children of the

Sun, she plays an important part. She is the great creator, who lives in the ancestral underworld, whither go the dead. Mother goddesses play an important part in all sorts of beliefs possessed by these peoples. The mother goddess is the Turquoise mother; she is the Spider Woman, the Salt Old Woman, the Maize Mother, and so forth : she fulfils functions similar to those fulfilled by the Great Mother of the Ancient East. The persistence of the mother goddess in such places is due to the fact that the community was evidently derived directly from the archaic civilization, and had many of its cultural elements, but, somehow or other, is no longer ruled over by the Children of the Sun. The Pueblo Indians now have no ruling class, so they have no cults of gods such as were found in Mexico, whence they certainly came. Therefore the original deity, the Great Mother, once more comes into prominence. This is markedly different to the sequence in communities where the ruling class changes its nature and its gods ; for in this case the mother goddess goes into the background. This shows that the nature of the religious system of any people can only be understood when its mode of origin from the archaic civilization is known.

The process of degradation of the culture of the archaic civilization can be watched very clearly among the Toradja of Central Celebes. Although visited by a Son of the

Sun, who married one of their women, they have no ruling class in the parts that he visited, for his sons went elsewhere to found chiefly houses. But he left his mark on their culture. He had taught them to cultivate plants, not by irrigation in this case, probably because he did not stay long enough, but by dry cultivation. He taught them many other things. When inquiry is made into their cults, it is found that these cults are performed, not by priests claiming descent from gods, but by priestesses who do not claim divine descent. These priestesses form a fraternity deriving its authority ultimately from the sky-world, that is, from the archaic civilization. It is said that, one day in the past, a woman was taken up to the sky-world and kept there until she had learned all the ritual of the Toradja priestesses, when she was sent back to earth. These priestesses concern themselves with agriculture, the curing of disease, death ceremonies, and house-building. Agriculture and house-building can certainly be put down to the account of the civilizers of the Toradja, for they certainly introduced both these things. Death ceremonies are almost certainly due to the influence of these people, for they are so similar throughout the world as to give reason to believe in their common origin in Egypt, which, as has been seen, was the great place of origin of ideas about the future life. The healing of disease might be thought to be a native craft in all parts

of the earth. But the ritual of the priestesses
in their leechcraft shows signs of its exotic
origin. It rests on the theory that the life
of a man is represented by his breath. It is
more or less independent of the body, and
can leave it during sleep. Death is due to
the permanent absence of the life. When
any one is ill, the aid of a priestess is sought.
She goes into a trance, and her " life " goes
to seek the absent " life " of the patient. It
may have been taken by an evil spirit, by a
ghost, or by a sky spirit. In the first two
cases, the priestess can return it. But when
a sky spirit has taken the life of the patient,
the " life " of the priestess, accompanied by a
familiar sky spirit, goes to the sky to ask for
its return. She may or may not be successful ;
the fate of the patient depends upon the success
or failure of her mission. The procedure of
Toradja leechcraft shows clearly that the ideas
must have been derived from the archaic
civilization. Australian " medicine-men " likewise derive their powers from the sky-world,
the home of the culture-heroes, and are able
to visit this place, which is inaccessible to
ordinary men.

In no cases where a culture-hero has visited
a people does he receive a cult. The All-
Fathers of the Australians, who have been
thought by some to represent the beginnings
of the notion of a supreme being, do not receive
any cult at all. They are just remembered
as the traditional culture bringers, who now

live up in the sky, whither the medicine-men can go. The crafts of the initiated priests and priestesses and the medicine-men are centred round practical matters, the healing of disease being prominent among them; and the craft is based on ideas handed down from the archaic civilization. More than that; it is, as will be shown in Chapter VIII, largely dependent on material givers of life left behind them by the people of the archaic civilization.

CHAPTER VII

LIFE AND IMMORTALITY

IN Egypt and Sumer the notion of the creation and procreation of human beings was composite, several independent elements having been incorporated one after the other to produce the final result. Apart from birth in the ordinary way, the creative crafts of the potter and the sculptor helped to frame the ideas of the earliest civilized men with regard to these topics. In particular the craft of the potter helped in the elaboration of the idea of the " mother pot," into which seed could be placed to grow, and this idea provided the foundation of the doctrine of reincarnation : the craft of the sculptor, regarded by the Egyptians as essentially creative, gave rise to the idea of the creation of men out of stone images ; and the funerary ritual provided the idea of the animation of such statues, thus perfecting the concept of creation of men out of stone images. The emergence of the Heliopolitan solar theology played an important part in emphasizing creative ideas. This theology tended to associate all life-giving powers with the sun-god,

and with the sky. This is natural : for, once
the attention of men had been paid to the
sun, it follows that the great powers of that
body would be recognized. The sun is the
great giver of life to the earth ; so, therefore,
the sky-world is the place of " life " and,
correspondingly, the underworld becomes the
place of " death." When the archaic civilization moved out from the Ancient East, it
therefore took with it notions of life-giving
attached to the sky-world rather than to the
earth. Consequently it is usually, though not
invariably, found, throughout the religious
systems of the world, that the creation of man
is the work of sky-gods, even in places where
no sun-cult now persists. Nevertheless, in
spite of this great revolution in thought, there
still persist, in the outlying parts of the earth,
mixed up with the ideas of the life-giving
powers of sky-beings, those still more primitive
ideas derived from pottery-making and metal-
working, by means of which the conception
of the creation of man was originally developed.
Thus, we find that in India, the great god
Brahma, originally a sun-god, created in the
same manner as Re, the god of Heliopolis in
Egypt ; he created by his voice, he produced
beings from his own body, just as Re. In
the Rig-Veda all life is said to come from the
sky ; man's soul is his breath, which at death
returns to the Sun. When the Sun wishes, he
draws out the life of a man, so that he dies.
At the same time, the creative crafts played their

part. Brahma created man like a blacksmith. Another creative god, Twashtri, developed the germ in the womb, and was the shaper of every form, human and animal:—"Twashtri has generated a strong man, a lover of the gods . . . Twashtri has created the whole world."

The history of thought is hard to understand in India, although there can be no doubt as to the foreign origin of its civilization. It is in the more outlying parts of the world, where movements of culture have been fewer, that the mode of derivation of ideas from the archaic civilization may best be understood. A good instance is that of the Toradja of Central Celebes. These people have been visited by one of the Children of the Sun, and have thus absorbed a certain amount of civilization. Since those early days they have been left comparatively undisturbed, so that complications do not arise. The tribes of the Toradja which have been studied best state that formerly the earth was devoid of inhabitants, so the gods decided to make men. The god of the sky and the goddess of the underworld ordered Pue mPalaburu, who was called "the kneader," "the smith," or "the man-maker," to make two images, man and woman, of stone, or perhaps, as some say, of wood. When he had done this, the god went to the sky to fetch the "breath of life" that was up there, the "eternal breath." While he was away, the goddess let the wind blow on the

images, and they were animated as mortals. The
god, Pue mPalaburu, who made the first images,
also makes each child in his smithy in the sky,
and then places it in its mother to be born.
The Toradja have learned iron-working from
the people of the archaic civilization. They
have also evidently learned from them the ideas
of creation connected with the creative crafts of
stone-carving and metal-working.

Pue mPalaburu is the only deity whose
name is known to the ordinary Toradja man
or woman. The other deities, including the
god of the sky and the goddess of the underworld, who played parts in the drama of creation,
are unknown except to the priestesses, the
members of a profession directly instituted
by the people of the sky-world. The reason
why Pue mPalaburu is remembered by every
one is obvious : he plays an important part in
the lives of all, in that he is their maker, to
whom they owe their very existence. Thus
it happens that sky-gods can persist after
the disappearance of the sun-cult, and of the
Children of the Sun, because of the relationship
that exists between these beings and every
member of the community. But this is only
re-stating, in another way, the general principle
that cults of gods are ancestor cults. For, in
a way, the respect paid to a creating god like
Pue mPalaburu is that paid to one's begettor.

The Toradja people do not belong to the
sky-world. They go at death to the underworld, a place ruled over by a goddess, obviously

one of the forms of the mother goddess, who thus receives her children back home once more. As has been mentioned, the creative crafts of the potter, the sculptor and the metal-worker are not logically associated with the sky-world : but, owing to the coming into prominence of the solar theology, they have been incorporated in that body of ideas. Consequently, there is produced, among the Toradja, the extraordinary paradox that, while the ghost of a man goes, after death, to the underworld, his life, which came from the sky, goes back to its source, and there remains, ready to be doled out to some baby just born. Thus the contrast in ideas as to the destiny of the human soul brought about in Egypt, when the Heliopolitans imposed themselves on the rest of Egypt as their sacred rulers, comes out in clear-cut fashion. It is perhaps still better shown in the island of Nias, situated west of Sumatra. The south part of this island is ruled over by a class of chiefs claiming descent from the sky-world. Every child in Nias gets its life from a god who lives in the sun. When a chief dies, his life, which is manifested in the breath, goes, together with his ghost, to the sky. When a commoner dies his ghost goes to the underworld, while his life, his breath, goes back to the god in the sun. The case of the chief shows that there is no essential difference between the destinations of the life and that of the ghost ; they can equally well go to the same place, but the circumstances in which the solar theology came into prominence are responsible for the remarkable state of affairs in which life and ghost can go to entirely different places.

The Australians have remembered their culture-heroes, who belonged to the sky-world, as givers of life :—" The Muramura Paralina when out hunting saw four unformed beings crouching together. He smoothed their bodies with his hands, stretched out their limbs, slit up their fingers and toes, formed a mouth, nose and eyes, stuck ears on, and otherwise turned them into mankind." In North America, likewise, the beings of the sky are the great givers of life. Among tribes who have practically no cults of deities, there still remains a belief in a Lord of Life who lives in the Sun.

Although the archaic civilization left as a legacy the idea that breath is life, and that this breath was in the sky, the native tribes were not always content to leave these ideas as they received them. I have pointed out that there is no essential relationship between " breath " as life and the sky. This came about through the peculiar circumstances of Egypt. So in some cases it has happened that his breath is associated with the underworld, where lives the great mother of men. The Pueblo Indians of North America believe that the Sun is the great creative power, from whom came all life. At the same time they believe that their ancestors were created, in the underworld, by the Great Mother. These tribes have stories of the Twin Children of the Sun, who were their culture-heroes, but they have no ruling class connected with the sky. The whole of their religious ideas are connected with the underworld. So when a man dies his ghost goes back to the hole in the ground where his ancestors emerged into this world, and returns by it to his ancestral underground home. His "breath body" follows the sun to the west, and there enters the underground land of the dead. Thus, although the solar association of the "life" persists in tradition, the connection with the underworld is still closer, and the "life" goes to join the ghost in the underworld.

The idea of sky-gods as givers of life explains why they persist in certain circumstances without any cult, often unknown to anyone except the priests. So long as the notion exists that they are the givers of life to each mortal, it seems certain that they will remain in memory, while those sky-gods who no longer have any direct connection with men are quickly forgotten.

The archaic civilization has left behind it the idea of reincarnation. This idea is found in various connections, but especially, in the case of the less civilized peoples, linked up with the social system of totemic clans. The political organization of the archaic civilization, from one end of the earth to the other, was based on a system of councils. Each major

unit of society managed its affairs by means of
a council. The ultimate unit of society was
the family. Then came the clan, the elders
of which met in council to discuss the business
of the clan. Above the clan in the social
hierarchy was the tribe or State, which was
governed by a council representing all the
clans. The council was usually presided over
by a member of the ruling group, if one existed,
but not by the Children of the Sun, who were
outside such a scheme, since they were concerned with the religious organization. Sometimes, as in North America, tribes joined into
confederacies, and each tribe sent its members
to sit, on terms of perfect equality, on a council
that transacted the affairs of the group.

This kind of political organization has been
left behind by the archaic civilization in various
parts of the world, and it is found in its most
typical form in Australia and North America.
An interesting feature of the council system
is that, in India, Indonesia, New Guinea,
Oceania, and in Europe, stone circles are used
for such meetings, the members of the council
sitting on the stones, or leaning against them.
Thus Stonehenge, which was situated in the
midst of the most thickly populated part of
England in those times, must have been the
great central meeting-place for a large region.
The stone circles were not exclusively used for
councils, but also for dancing, and other ceremonials. In New Guinea they are used for
cannibal feasts.

We are not concerned here directly with
the practice of holding council meetings, but
with the inner constitution of the clan itself,
for this constitution has certain features that
have exercised the minds of men for many
years. Each clan consists of a number of
men and women, who claim common descent.
Moreover, each clan possesses an emblem, an
animal, plant, or material object, to which it
attaches particular importance. Great respect
is paid to this emblem. If an animal or plant,
it must not be eaten by the members of the
clan to which it is attached; if a material
object, it must be used with great ceremony.
Sometimes the animal is claimed as the ancestor
of the clan. The emblem is usually called
a *Totem*, and the form of social organization
consisting of clans with totems is called *Totemism*. It has long been thought that totemism
was a native product of some place such as
Australia, for it. exists among these lowly
people. But, in Australia, and in North
America, the two most important centres of
totemism, the culture-heroes are said to have
organized the tribes on this basis, and to have
taught the people the necessary ceremonies
for initiation into the clan. This suggests that
the institution of " totemism " was part of the
archaic civilization, and all that is known
of the constitution of the totemic clan goes
to support this conclusion.

It is not hard to show that the people of
the archaic civilization were intimately con-

nected with animals. This has already been
done for Egypt, where the nomes had animals,
plants, and material objects for ensigns, where,
also, the animals of the nomes were intimately
connected with the gods and with the rulers
of the nomes. In Indonesia it can be shown
that the people of the archaic civilization were
intimately connected with certain animals,
such as crocodiles, apes, fowls, pigs, cats and
dogs. In particular cases, classes of the community, chiefs, priests and so forth, who have
been derived from the archaic civilization,
are not allowed to eat certain of these animals,
or actually claim to be descended from them.
It is also believed that these animals differ
from other animals in that they have a "life"
similar to that of man. Since the idea of the
"life" is so intimately connected with the
people of the sky-world, the belief that animals
have a "life" like that of men is further
evidence pointing to the belief, on the part
of the people of the archaic civilization, in a
relationship between men and certain animals.
Moreover, the natives tell tales about punish-
ments meted out to villages because they
laughed at certain of these animals. The
Toradja of Celebes, for instance, say that a
woman, sewing in her house, dropped a needle
through the floor, and sent the cat down to
get it. When the animal returned, all the
people laughed at it, whereupon the village
was turned to stone, and covered by the waters
of the lake. The point of the story is that

the powers of petrifaction, and of causing floods, were ascribed to the people of the archaic civilization, who evidently were considered to punish in this way acts of rudeness towards those animals with which they claimed some sort of relationship.

When a careful examination is made of the ideas as to the manner of perpetuation of totemic clans, a very remarkable fact becomes evident ; and, curiously enough, this fact can best be observed in Australia. The Australian tribes are practically universally organized in totemic clans, though the social organization of some tribes represents a later stage of development than that of others. But if the tribes with the earlier form of social organization, those with mother-right, be observed, it will be found that they believe that their totemic clans persist by virtue of a self-perpetuating mechanism. The Urabunna, a tribe of Central Australia, state that, in the old days, the Alcheringa times as they are called, the ancestors of the different totemic clans lived as a number of half-human, half-animal or plant people. No one can suggest how they arose. Those ancestors left behind them spirit individuals, which have continually been undergoing reincarnation. When a man dies, he becomes a spirit, and enters another woman. These spirit individuals are supposed to inhabit certain spots, sometimes only one kind at a spot, sometimes two or three kinds. Each person is, therefore, the living incarnation of an original

spirit individual that emanated somehow from
an Alcheringa ancestor.

It has been claimed that this curious idea
of reincarnation shows that the Australians
had no knowledge of conception, and that
they invented this idea to account for facts.
But the Australians themselves refer the inception of the system to the days of the culture-
heroes, and do not pretend to understand how
it arose. Therefore it is to the times of the
archaic civilization that reference must be
made for further information.

The idea of reincarnation is widespread.
It occurs in connection with totemic clans
in North America. The Yuchi of the Savannah
River, who call themselves Children of the
Sun, and believe that they go to the sky after
death, say that each person is the reincarnation
of a maternal ancestor. Each child is named
after a maternal grandparent's brother or
sister; paternal grandparents do not enter
into the matter at all. The child is not named
for four days after birth, because it is thought
that it takes four days for the ghost to get to
the land of the dead, and thus, presumably,
that it takes the same time for the spirit of
the ancestor to get to the child that it is to
occupy. The Huron also believed in reincarnation, for they used to bury the bodies of
little children by the roadside, in the hope that
they would enter passing women and thus be
born. They also possessed a set of names for
each clan, all derived from characteristics of

the clan totem, from which names the council
women of the clan chose one for each child.

When it is remembered that the sky-beings
who came as culture-heroes among the Australians were life-givers, a ready explanation is
forthcoming for the existence, among such
peoples, of the doctrine of reincarnation. The
potter and other craft gods were able to make
spirit individuals of the necessary type, and
to place them in the proper position to be
born. Further, the notion of the mother-
pot, so widespread as it has become throughout
the world, helps further to understand how
it came to be agreed that seed could be placed
in women to be fertilized. The idea that spirits
could enter women to be born was common
in old times in India. Stories are told of the
transference of an unborn child from one
woman to another. Stories are also told of the
manner by which gods entered women to be
reborn. Such stories are commonplace in
the Indian Epics. Thus the notion of reincarnation is not confined to the totemic clan
system; it has simply become bound up with
it, owing to historical circumstances.

It is natural that man, having been engaged,
since the beginnings of civilization, in devising
means for his own ends, should, the world over,
eagerly adopt, from the archaic civilization,
whatever tended to prolong his life, or to give
him hope of immortality, when once that
hope had been extended to him. The precipi-

tate that, in all parts of the world, testifies to
the former presence of the archaic civilization,
is, as has been seen, composed of customs and
beliefs that centre round the interests of
man, and are not concerned with abstract
things. To the list already formed may be
added the doctrine of immortality that is bound
up, in all parts of the world, with the idea
of a ritual death and rebirth.

The ancient Greeks, the Romans, and other
peoples of the centuries just prior to our era
possessed religious systems, called Mysteries
after their secret character, the members of
which looked forward to immortal life in the
hereafter (1) All mystery religions have similar features. They are founded on the story
of the death of a god, and his resurrection
through the offices of his mother, the great
goddess. The young god has different names,
Tammuz in Babylonia, Attis in Syria, Adonis
among the Greeks. He is associated, in each
case, with a mother goddess, such as Ishtar,
Cybele, and Aphrodite. Another famous god
of mysteries was Mithra, associated with the
goddess Anahita. In the Isis mysteries the
god was Osiris. The initiate to the society
had to undergo, like the god himself, a
form of death. Prior to this he had to
fast and to submit to tortures, in imita-
tion of the sufferings of the god himself.
Then he was shown certain sacred objects;
in the case of the mysteries of Eleusis a head
of corn. He was then subjected to a process

of ritual death and rebirth, and thus was supposed to have acquired the gift of immortality. The societies were usually in grades, and the novice had to advance one step at a time, just as in a Freemason Lodge. At each grade he received a new name, often that of an animal, and it is supposed that he wore the skin of an animal, or a mask to represent the animal, on certain ceremonial occasions. It is natural that the mysteries, being secret, should be so little known, and that the details of the ritual can usually only be surmised.

The central feature of the ritual was the ceremonial death and rebirth which gave immortality. There is no logical connection between the two ideas : there is no rational reason why death and rebirth should lead to immortality. The relationship can only, it seems, satisfactorily be explained on the assumption that the ritual was derived ultimately from that of the mummification of Osiris in Egypt, by means of which the dead gained immortal life. In the case of the mysteries there was no need to perform that part of the ritual ; all that was necessary was to simulate the death and resurrection. The initiate had to " die," and then rise again with a new name. He was then immortal.

The mystery religions bear witness to the real preoccupations of men, for they alone have survived the shocks of fortune. When it is remembered that the central idea of these organizations was elaborated at a very early

stage of human society ; when it is remembered
that some of these organizations have persisted
through several phases of development of
religious systems ; then it is evident that
their tenacity is due to their appeal to a fundamental human trait.

One of the best known of the mystery religions
was connected with Mithra, an old Persian sun-
god, who belongs to the period before the
reform of Zoroaster, which brought into being
the religious system now known as Parsi-ism (2).
He is mentioned in the Vedas of India, as
well as in the Avesta of Persia, being one of
the few gods who survived the separation of
the two religious systems. Zoroaster, who
was nearly a monotheist, turned the sun-god
into a supreme being of justice and truth,
and evidently tried to ignore Mithra, who was
also a god of justice and truth. But, as can be
told from the large number of nobles of his
time who bore names compounded of Mithra,
forces were too strong for him, and the ancestral
Mithra cult held its own. Some of these
Mithra-named nobles went to Asia Minor, and
there kept up the ancestral Mithra-cult, and
mixed it with Babylonian star-worship. When
the Romans got to Asia Minor, they took
over this form of religion : first of all the
soldiers of the army adopted it ; then traders
from Asia Minor disseminated it throughout
the Roman Empire ; and Asia Minor slaves
brought it with them and made local shrines ;
finally, in the second century A.D. Mithraism

became the cult of the court at Rome. At the time when Christianity was conquering the lands round the Mediterranean, Mithraism had taken firm hold of the Roman Empire, so that a map of Mithra monuments throughout the Roman Empire defines the principal towns and stations. This could only happen when the appeal of the cult went far beyond that of the ordinary cult of a god, such as the sun-cult, which does not promise any hopes of immortality. Although the cult of Mithra was formerly in the hands of nobles and kings, it ultimately became that of the ordinary man, who eagerly embraced its tenets, and followed the god of justice and truth in the hope of a blessed immortality.

If this great doctrine of the immortal benefits to be derived from a process of ritual death and rebirth became so deeply rooted in the Mediterranean, the home of new developments of thought; if this movement was able to survive the intellectual outburst of Greek thought, it should have survived in other parts of the world, wherever, in fact, the old seekers after the earthly paradise settled to exploit the resources of the country. A study of the initiation ceremonies of totemic clans, and of the ritual of secret societies, shows that these ceremonies correspond, often in detail, to those of the Mysteries of the Ancient East; and when the detailed study is made of mysteries throughout the world, it will probably be found that the ceremonies of communities

such as those of the Australians will throw a
flood of light on those of the Egyptians and
other peoples. These ceremonies are very
important in the life of each boy, for by them
he becomes a man, and is made into a full
member of the tribe. Part of the ritual includes
a simulated death and reanimation. Among
the Kurnai tribe of Australia, for instance, the
boys, during the initiation ceremonies, were
" put to sleep " at night, and woke the next
day as men.

The North American Indians still preserve,
or did so until late years, ceremonies which
clearly reveal the relationship between a ritual
death and rebirth and immortality. The
mystery society of the Ojibwa has been closely
studied by Hoffman (3). It was founded by
a sky-spirit, through a mediator named the
Great Rabbit. The Great Rabbit looked down
on earth from the sky, and saw how ignorant
men were. So he instructed the Otter in the
mysteries, and gave him the sacred rattle,
drum and tobacco. He made a lodge and
taught the otter all the secrets, and with a
bag containing cowrie shells " shot " him, so
that he might have immortality, and be able
to convey the secrets to his kinsmen. Much
of the old teaching has been lost, but enough
is known of it to enable some picture of the
proceedings to be formed. The novice is
instructed by the priest prior to his initiation
into the first of the four grades of the society.
He has to take a sweat-bath, and there is

visited by the priest, who shows him certain
bags and their magical contents. When he
goes into the lodge for the ceremony, the
Supreme Being is supposed to be there. The
candidate has to stand up, and is approached
by a priest with a bag of mink skin containing
shells, pigments, effigies, amulets, and so forth.
The priest "shoots" him with the bag, and
he has to fall down apparently lifeless. The
priests then lay bags with givers of life on
his back, and he finally "coughs up" certain
small shells shaped like cowries. He then
tries to rise, but is unable for some time to do
so. Finally he succeeds, and is then become
a member of the first grade of the society.

The decision to join the society is the result
of an experience which each boy has at
some time or other. He goes out into the
wilds, fasts, and after a time has a vision.
If this be of a bear, he kills a bear and wears
one of its claws for an amulet, believing that
the bear will always protect him, an idea that
evidently lay at the back of the custom of
wearing bears' claws in the Upper Palæolithic
Age. When he becomes a member of the
society, he has an image of a bear in his magical
bag. Another primitive trait is shown by the
practices of these men. For members of the
first degree of the society try to obtain hunters'
"medicines," consisting of pictures of animals
with the heart depicted, and coated with a
small amount of vermilion. In this they are also
acting like the men of the Upper Palæolithic Age.

When a man wishes to advance to the second and later degree he has to undergo like ceremonies of purification and preparation. After he has joined the second division, he is able to change himself into his guardian animal, say a bear; his heart is supposed to be full of magical power; and he can see or act at a distance. The ritual death and rebirth is a constant feature of the initiation into each stage. In the third degree use is made of ginseng, " man root," which is supposed to be of " divine " origin. This is interesting in view of the great importance attached by the Cherokee and other Indian tribes, as well as by the Chinese, to this root. " The . . . spirit taught us to do right. He gave us life and told us how to prolong it. These things he taught us, and gave us roots for medicine." Those who have passed into the third stage become powerful magicians, who derive their power from the sky, and often have sky spirits for " familiars." In the fourth division power is given to communicate with the spirits of dead members of the society, and to learn hidden secrets.

It is not surprising, since the central idea of the secret societies of the world is based on the conception of the derivation of immortality from ceremonial death and rebirth, to find that the ritual of the Ojibwa society, as well as of other societies among tribes of North America, has been compared with that of the Book of the Dead in Egypt, and that identity

between the two has been asserted to exist (4).
The probable derivation of the ritual from
Egyptian funerary practice makes it clear
why the cult of the dead is so prominent in
the rites of secret societies in Melanesia and
elsewhere. This derivation explains many
things. For instance, one of the chief aims of
the ritual of mummification is that of holding
intercourse with the dead ; the king animates
the portrait statue of his father, and can thus
communicate with him. Likewise, the members
of the secret society can communicate with their
dead.

The ceremonies of initiation into totemic
clans and into secret societies are of the utmost
importance for the study of the history of
early civilization. For in these organizations
are to be sought the esoteric wisdom handed
on from the archaic civilization. In every
case the inception of the organization, whatever
it may be, is ascribed to beings who can easily
be identified as men of the archaic civilization.
By means of these secret fraternities, whether
of the clan or of the secret society, the knowledge of medicine, of magic and of the history
of the tribe, is handed on from generation
to generation. The ritual death and rebirth
serves to make a man into a new individual,
as well as to give him immortality. The
young man who is initiated into his clan, the
novice who enters a society, is given a new
name, and is thereby supposed to have become
someone else. He then knows things hidden

from the women, the children, and the non-
initiates. The secrecy with which knowledge
was preserved and handed on to the privileged
few, was an important feature of early civilization. Even to-day it is still practised where
any advantage is to be gained. The great
prestige of the people of the archaic civilization
can still better be appreciated when we remem-
ber that their knowledge, which certainly was
considerable, seeing that they understood the
value of sweat-baths and of massage as thera-
peutical methods, was handed on from generation to generation as a privilege, and not
as a right. The mysterious wrappings that
surround secret societies in all places throw
light on the doings of the early ruling groups,
who deliberately, it would seem, kept to themselves the knowledge that gave them their
position and power, and only allowed those
to participate who had been properly prepared
by preliminary purification for the privilege.
(*See* Appendix.)

CHAPTER VIII

GIVERS OF LIFE

ONE of the profoundest and most wide-spread effects of the archaic civilization on the beliefs and practices of men throughout the world has been in the realm of magic. No one who reads the accounts of the beliefs and practices of the Egyptians and Babylonians can fail to be impressed with the great importance paid by these peoples to the use of givers of life of various sorts. Although the rulers of Egypt were incarnate deities, yet they were in great degree dependent on various objects for protection. The Pharaoh wore his crown with the vulture and the uræus. His regalia was all highly charged with magical power; he was given magical power by the god Re, his father, and he could transmit this power to his son or to his statues. " Egyptian magic " is a household phrase, the persistence of which testifies to the prestige of these people in this department of life. Small wonder, therefore, that, when Egyptian civilization began to influence the world, magical ideas took deep root among native peoples,

especially when it is remembered that the
practice of magic, using that term to mean
the use of Givers of Life, of whatever sort,
goes right back to the beginnings of human
society. From India right across to America
the practice of magic is closely associated
with the archaic civilization; we find the
magicians of India practising the mango trick,
that trick whereby a man causes a mango
plant apparently to grow into full maturity
in the course of a few minutes; the ancient
Polynesian magicians had the same power
of illusion; and the medicine-men of American
Indian tribes have on countless occasions
persuaded critical European spectators that they
have similar powers over maize plants. The
knowledge of these ceremonies is, in North
America, and other places, part of the hidden
lore belonging to the secret societies of the
various tribes, and the constitution of these
societies betrays their origin in the archaic
civilization. Fraternities of magicians have
evidently spread across the world, having their
origin, it seems, in Egypt, the home of the
archaic civilization. Whatever attitude be taken
towards the trick of making a plant grow in a
few minutes, or that of bringing the " dead "
to life, or any other wonderful feat, whether
any credence be placed in them, or whether
it simply be said that the practitioner has
a wonderful power of illusion, it is nevertheless
patent that the power of persuading intelligent
Europeans that the trick has been performed,

so that they are unable to detect the illusion, is, in itself, remarkable. Small wonder, therefore, that the founders of the archaic civilization, who had knowledge of that sort, were remembered all over the world as marvellous men, for they certainly were marvellous compared with the native food-gatherers with whom they had to deal. So, when reading native traditions to the effect that the Children of the Sun could fly through the air, and could perform other wonderful feats, it is to be remembered that Australian medicine-men are credited with similar powers, and that these feats may have some substantial basis of presumed fact behind them. The people of the archaic civilization, or, at least, the magicians and rulers, may have been able to persuade their subjects that they could fly, or perform other wonderful deeds.

The fame of the people of old was so great that all objects left behind by them, or things with which they were especially associated, are regarded, by their successors, as gifted with magical powers, and as good to use for the curing of disease, for agriculture, for warding off harm, and for other purposes. The most widespread and the most prominent of all these objects is the polished stone celt, the characteristic implement of the archaic civilization from Ireland to America. Wherever it is found, it is certain that this civilization has exerted its influence. For the polished stone celt was only made in definite cultural circumstances. It is not an implement that was

invented independently by different peoples,
for the men of the Palæolithic Age lived for
tens of thousands of years and never thought
of making it. What is more, its use only
persisted for a short time, and it disappeared
when metals came into general use.

Even to-day, in Europe, the polished stone
celt is regarded as an amulet. Listen to the
ideas held about it in Jutland. "The thunderstone falls down from the sky in thunder-
storms or, more accurately, whenever the
lightning strikes. The stroke of the lightning,
according to this view, consists in the descent
of the stone, and the flash and the thunder-
clap are mere after effects or secondary
phenomena."

The stone protects the house in which it is
kept against strokes of lightning : "where it
has once struck it is not worth coming again."
In many parts the stone was simply kept
lying on a shelf, on a chest of drawers, or in a
box. Usually, however, it was kept in a
particular place where it might be free from
daily disturbance : it was immured in the wall,
laid under the floor, on the top of the four-
post bedstead, or under the roof. The object
was evidently to avoid touching the thunderstone, and this is sometimes very distinctly
emphasized in the records ; thus, in Jutland,
it was often kept under the far side of the fixed
bedstead.

"The thunderstone keeps trolls and other
pernicious creatures from the house, and as

most of the evils which befall man and his property are due, according to the old popular belief, to witchcraft and evil beings, the thunderstone in general becomes a protection for house and cattle, it draws luck to the house, can be used as a healing power, and so on. This idea particularly asserted itself in certain cases where an injurious influence, the origin of which was unknown, was frequently felt. Thus the thunderstone particularly protects the little unchristened child against being 'changed' and the horse in the stall stable against 'nightmare.' But it was especially common to use the thunderstone as a protection against mishaps with the milk and its treatment; it was laid on the milk-shelves that the milk might keep fresh or give better cream, and put on the churn that the churning might give good butter" (1). Even in this country these implements are used for good luck. In India they are constantly used on altars in connection with the cult of the mother goddess. In Indonesia they are prized as heirlooms by various chiefs in Borneo, Celebes, and Sumba, in places, therefore, where they are no longer made. Many such implements are found in British New Guinea, in the gold gravels of the mountains. The natives of New Guinea do not make them, except in the Geelvink Bay region of Dutch New Guinea, but they consider them as powerful in magic, and use them for various purposes connected with agriculture, healing, and fishing.

Stone celts are not regarded as magical by peoples who use them : for instance, in Australia, Polynesia and North America ; the belief is confined to the countries where their use is a thing of the past. This shows that the power is not ascribed to the objects in themselves, but because of their associations.

Second only perhaps to the cult of the stone celt, all the world over, is that of some form of crystal, especially of quartz. Even such a primitive people as the Punan of Borneo, who are still in the food-gathering stage, use quartz in their magic. " The Punan has great faith in charms, especially for bringing good luck in hunting. He usually carries, tied to his quiver, a bundle of small objects which have forcibly attracted his attention for any reason, e.g. a large quartz crystal, a strangely shaped tusk or tooth or pebble, etc., and the bundle of charms is dipped in the blood of the animals that fall to his blow-pipe." Notice that these men use teeth and dip the charms in blood : two customs apparently closely connected with those of the people of the Upper Palæolithic Age in Europe. These customs have already been discussed (see pp. 5, 7). It now remains to account for the quartz. The Kayan, who also live in Borneo near the Punan, but are much higher than them in culture, also have bundles of charms, one to each village. " This bundle, which is the property of the whole household or village, generally contains hair taken from the heads that hang in the gallery ;

a crocodile's tooth ; the blades of a few knives
that have been used in special ceremonies ;
a few crystals or pebbles of strange shapes ;
pigs' teeth of unusual shape (of both wild
and domestic pig), feathers of a fowl . . .
stone axe-heads called the teeth of Balingo, and
isang, i.e. palm leaves that have been put to
ceremonial use." Here, again, are animals' teeth,
in addition to stone celts and quartz. The
peoples of British New Guinea also use small
bits of quartz in their magic. According to
Prof. Seligman (*The Melanesians of British
New Guinea*, p. 174): " Certain charm stones—
as far as my knowledge goes these are always
of quartz—are so highly charged with magical
power that it is not considered safe for them to
be touched with the hand." In Australia
likewise quartz plays a very prominent part in
magic. The magicians derive their power from
the beings of the sky-world, that is from the
people of the archaic civilization. Howitt
(*The Native Tribes of South-East Australia*,
pp. 357-8) says, " In all the tribes I refer to (these
cover the whole of the south-east part of the
continent) there is a belief that the medicine-
men (magicians of the tribe) can project substances in an invisible manner into their victims.
One of the principal projectives is said to be
quartz, especially in the crystallized form.
Such quartz crystals are always, in many
parts of Australia, carried as part of the stock-
in-trade of the medicine-men, and are usually
carefully concealed from sight, especially of

women, but are exhibited to the novices at
the initiation ceremonies."

In all parts of North America we find likewise the belief in the great power of quartz
crystals as givers of life. They usually form
the chief object in the paraphernalia of the
magician.

The explanation of this world-wide appreciation of quartz, and of crystals of similar
colour, lies in the fact that the spread of the
archaic civilization was due to the search for
various substances, prominent among which
was gold. Quartz is the matrix of gold. The
countries where quartz is looked upon as a
giver of life contain traces of the people of the
archaic civilization, usually in the form of
stone remains or of ancient mining works.
In Australia the evidence for the past existence
of the people of the archaic civilization is
mainly traditional, the use of stone celts being
the most important material witness. But
in British New Guinea there are ample traces
of the working of gold at some time in the
past. The gold-miners worked quartz, and
made implements of it. The present-day natives
do not do so : on the other hand, they attach
great importance to it as a giver of life. It
therefore seems that the natives have transferred to quartz, the stone in which they knew
the gold-miners were interested, the ideas
that the gold-seekers attached to gold. If
gold-seekers came to Australia they would go
to places where they found quartz, and the

association could easily arise in the minds of the natives between those wonderful men and the stone that they so highly prized. Or else it may be that the gold-miners themselves looked upon quartz as a giver of life, because it was the matrix of gold. The ancient Egyptians, and other peoples of the Ancient East, certainly used quartz in their magic, for amulets and so forth.

Crystal has always been high in the estimation of alchemists and others interested in the fancied magical properties of givers of life. In whatever way the matter be explained, the great preoccupation of the people of the archaic civilization accounts readily for the magical powers ascribed to quartz by so many peoples. Thus the prime motive of the outward movement of civilization from Egypt has had important results upon the beliefs of widely scattered peoples.

In yet other ways have the people of the archaic civilization influenced profoundly the beliefs and practices of the peoples of the regions in which they settled. It is curious to see how that the manner of contact between the people of the archaic civilization and the native tribes has apparently determined the lines upon which native thought should develop. For example, the gold-miners of the past in British New Guinea have left behind them many objects of stone, which are regarded by the native tribes as potent in magic. We hear, for instance, of a native in possession

of a circular stone mortar, from which he
would not be parted lest harm should come.
The original use of the mortar was quite unknown
to its owner. The natives also possess stone
pestles which they look upon as charms. A
small stone image is carried by the natives
from place to place and put into the ground
to give good yam crops, which is significant
when it is remembered that the people of the
archaic civilization in all probability introduced
agriculture to all parts of the world. The
natives of British New Guinea also use, for
their magical practice, stone of the kinds of
rock of which the people of the archaic civilization made their implements, of mica-schist, sand-
stone, volcanic rock, diabase, diorite, granite,
quartz, hornblende, ophicalcite, obsidian and
so forth. This is another instance of the
transference of supposed power from one object
to another that resembles it.

A fishing charm of these people is of interest.
An irregularly fractured piece of quartz which
is connected with a short piece of string with
a string knot to which are attached five small
netted string bags containing charms and two
other charm objects. The latter are a piece
of resin and an irregularly fractured piece
of jasper, or jasper-like rock. The five netted
bags contain respectively a highly-polished
pebble, a clam (*Tridacna*) pearl, two clam
pearls, fragments of resin, a fragment of quartz,
all of them objects well known as " givers of
life." In all probability the settlements of

the people of the archaic civilization were partly determined in British New Guinea by the presence of pearls, so the natives probably derived their use of pearls from the same source as they derived that of quartz.

In Torres Straits, between British New Guinea and Australia, stones, often in the form of human images, play an important part in ceremonies, especially those for the production of rain and yams. Indeed, the magic of these peoples is centred mainly round old carved and painted stones, which formerly were numerous, but now have mostly disappeared. The islands of the eastern group of Torres Straits obtained most of their culture from the western group : many of the natural and worked sacred stones in the Murray Islands are of foreign origin, and there can be no doubt that the majority of these must have come from the western islands. This shows that stones were being carried about for the purpose of magic. The origin of these stones is lost in the past, and they are undoubtedly remnants of the archaic civilization.

The people of Torres Straits also use clam shells in their magic and this, again, points to the archaic civilization as the source of givers of life used in magical practice.

Much has been written about the magical practice of the peoples of Melanesia. Cordington was the first to call attention to the subject, in his book on *The Melanesians* :— " The Melanesian mind is entirely possessed by the belief in a supernatural power or influence, called almost universally *mana*. This is what works to effect everything which is beyond the ordinary power of men, outside the common processes of nature; it is present in the atmosphere of life, attaches itself to persons and to things, and is manifested by results which can only be ascribed to its operation . . . But this power, though itself impersonal, is always connected with some person. If a stone is found to have a supernatural power, it is because a spirit has associated itself with it." *Mana* is the dominant feature of the culture of southern Melanesia. There it is associated with certain spirits called *vui*, who are apparently the traditional representatives of the sacred chiefs of the archaic civilization. These *vui* have much *mana* and are closely associated with stones. In the Banks Islands and New Hebrides: "The spirits who are approached with . . . offerings are almost always connected with stones to which the offerings are made. Such stones have some of them been sacred to some spirit from ancient times, and the knowledge of the way to approach the spirit has been handed down to the man who now possesses it." Again we are told of these *vui*: "In the Banks Islands and in the Northern New Hebrides the purely spiritual beings who are incorporeal are innumerable and unnamed. These are they whose representative form is generally stone, who haunt the places that are sacred because of their presence, and who connect themselves with certain snakes, owls, sharks, and other creatures." In their relationship with animals these spirits show again their nature; they belong to the archaic civilization. In Egypt it was found that the making of portrait statues was associated with the divine kings, and that the king could transfer to his statue the *sa*, or magic fluid, that he got from the Sun-god himself. It is found that, in Melanesia, the *mana* is associated closely with old stone images and also with stones of peculiar shape. When a man finds a stone that he thinks is full of *mana*, he tries to find out by means of dreams if it be the abode of a spirit. If it is, then he uses it to get rain, good crops, and so on.

The Egyptian customs give the clue to those of Melanesia. For the people of the archaic civilization in any region would believe that the portrait statues which they made were full of magical power, and could be animated by the ghost of the original. So when the ruling family died out the peoples would still continue to use whatever remains they had left behind them that were of use in this way, and their attention would beyond doubt be fixed especially upon the stone statues, full of the magic power of their originals. The supply of such statues would in time give out, and the people then would tend to choose out stones of certain shapes, and would test their choice by dreaming.

The part of Melanesia where we find the

belief in *mana* most highly developed, the
northern New Hebrides and the Banks Islands,
is full of remains of the archaic civilization.
Much stonework has been discovered in these
islands, and dolmens are still used on ceremonial
occasions. It is therefore highly significant
to find that the magical practice of these people
is centred round the remains of the archaic
civilization. Further, the people of this region
are said to have practically no " religion."
That is explained by the fact that the original
representatives of the *vui* spirits have gone, and
have left their remembrance only in association
with certain material objects. The *vui* have
no descendants to carry on their cult, so there
is no " religion."

The practices of the people of Ponape in the
Carolines, where are tremendous ruins of the
archaic civilization, form a connecting link
between those of Egypt and Melanesia. Ponape
is said to have been built by men who came
from Yap, further west in Micronesia, floating
on stones, and they built Ponape where the
stones stranded on the reef. In Ponape it
is said that certain spirits came from the sky
and turned into stones (an idea obviously
derived from the making of portrait statues,
which was practised by the early people of
Ponape). The gods can only be approached
through these stones, just as, in Egypt, the
ghost of the dead king, the god himself, was
approached through his stone statue. These
stones had power as givers of life, and only

the sacred king of Ponape could practise the rites connected with them.

The custom of transporting stones from one settlement seems to have been universal among the people of the archaic civilization. From Indonesia right to the furthest confines of the Pacific we find that the users of stone took great stones with them to set up as monuments in their new homes. This is seen clearly in the eastern Pacific, where is the great *marae*, or pyramidal building of Raiatea near Tahiti, the religious centre of the great region round about. When a new *marae* or pyramid was to be built anywhere, a stone was brought from the *marae* of Raiatea, evidently so that the sanctity of the old might be transferred to the new building.

The practices of the Melanesians and the people of Torres Straits can thus readily be understood as having been derived directly from the archaic civilization. If, therefore, we compare Melanesia, New Guinea and Australia, we find that the material objects chosen out by the people for their magical practices are intimately connected with the archaic civilization. In New Guinea the actual stone remains are so used, as well as pearls, for which the ancients were diving ; in Australia, on the other hand, the magic centres mainly round quartz. The Australians also use much human fat in their magic, which can be explained on the hypothesis that the people of the archaic civilization practised cannibalism, and attached

magical virtue to human flesh and blood.
But the Australians do not use stones for their
magic, nor do they seem, so far as I am aware,
to regard their polished stone implements as
thunderstones. This absence of interest in
stones can be accounted for on the assumption
that the magic of the Australians has not been
influenced profoundly by the people of the
archaic civilization, who have left behind them
no stone images in that continent. The Australians therefore would be quite unaware of
any possible magical power residing in certain
stones on account of their use as stone statues
that could be animated. Otherwise it seems
to me to be impossible to explain this fact.
The magic of Melanesia, on the other hand,
shows every sign of the influence of the archaic
civilization.

All the available evidence points to the
archaic civilization as the source of the magic
of the peoples of North America. The use
of quartz has already been cited in connection
with the gold-mining activities of these people.
The Indian tribes invariably ascribe the beginnings of their magic to their culture-heroes,
to the Children of the Sun, or to the Ancestral
Animals, who often lived in the sky, and therefore belonged to the archaic civilization (see
p. 109). The Indians possess what are called
" medicine-bags," which are filled with all
manner of objects regarded as magical. It
is noteworthy that, in the case of tribes near
Mexico, the seat of the parent civilizations of

the north part of the continent, the bags contain small stone images, that are regarded as beings gifted with great powers. The Pueblo Indians have many of these images, usually of jade, most of which are of animals, whose origin is unknown, but whose workmanship strongly suggests Mexican influence. Most of these bags contain parts of animals that enter into the totemic system, which can therefore act as protectors.

In some cases it is possible to detect direct traces of the archaic civilization. The Omaha, a Sioux tribe of the Plains, who have lost much of their original culture in the course of migration, have still retained some secret societies, and also some very powerful " givers of life," of whose origin they are ignorant. Perhaps the most important object is the Sacred Shell. No one knows what it stands for, but every one holds it in a superstitious dread; in all the tribe there is no person exempt from fear of this shell. The superstition that clings about it indicates that its rites relate to the cosmic forces and to fundamental beliefs relative to life and death. Among the Osage branch of the Omaha the shell is associated with the introduction of life on the earth. This shell is a specimen of the *Unio Alatus*, the pearl-bearing mussel, a specimen known to occur only in the Ohio, Missouri and northern Mississippi and in the Great Lakes.

It has already been said that the original

population of the United States built mounds,
often pyramidal in shape, and that these
mounds are concentrated near rivers and in
places where gold existed. The mound-builders
were seeking pearls among other things, for
immense numbers have been found in the
mounds. Since thousands were placed with
the dead in urns, they must have been put
in the grave to act as "givers of life." It
is known that the ancestors of the Omaha
came out of this mound-building area. So
the great importance attached by the Omaha
to the pearl-bearing mussel can be explained
when the history of the tribe is known. This
is a striking instance of the principle that
men are really interested in the supposed life-
giving properties of an object, not in the manner
by which it came to acquire its properties.

Another illuminating instance of a giver of
life that obviously has been acquired from
the archaic civilization, is that of the cowrie
shell, used in the ritual of the Ojibwa society
of the Mide'wiwin, which has been described
in the last chapter. The ceremonial killing
and bringing to life of the candidate is performed by means of a shell shaped like a cowrie,
sometimes by an actual cowrie shell. Since
the cowrie shell does not exist in America, the
nearest source of supply being Hawaii, it is
evident that the use of this shell must have
been introduced, and the introducers were,
according to native tradition, connected with the
sky-world, that is, with the archaic civilization.

What was the magical practice of the food-gathering tribes of the outlying parts of the earth before the coming of the archaic civilization ? It is not easy at present to give an answer to that question. But it may, indeed, be questioned whether they had any at all. Judging from the paraphernalia of a food-gathering people like the Punan of Borneo, it seems possible that all the objects used in magic by them were acquired from the archaic civilization. We find blood, teeth of animals and quartz as the chief magical objects used by those people. It might be claimed that the Punan had, like the people of the Upper Palæolithic Age, already come independently to use teeth and blood as givers of life, and that they had acquired the use of quartz from their neighbours. Good support for this explanation lies in the fact that the use of blood and teeth, having been present from very early times, responds to some deep-seated tendencies of human beings, for the use of these objects was derived from fundamental experiences of life. On the other hand, it is possible that this very appeal would have caused a food-gathering people like the Punan, who perhaps had no givers of life at all, to choose out blood and teeth from the paraphernalia of more richly endowed peoples.

The presence of teeth and blood in the magical practice of the Punan, therefore, of itself, constitutes little as evidence of the tendency of such people to acquire magical objects

independently of other peoples. The magical
practice of the Australians likewise seems to
have been wholly acquired from the archaic
civilization, and there seems to be very little
scope for the possibility of native invention.
It is therefore quite possible that the use of
givers of life had an origin, in the days of the
Upper Palæolithic Age, in the brain of one man,
and that the whole of the magical practice of
the world has been derived thence. Certainly
it is quite easy, when the mode of development
of the use of givers of life be called to mind,
to realize that this could have happened.
The further we can penetrate into the past,
the clearer does it become, to the unbiassed
mind, that the whole development, in the
Ancient East certainly, was perfectly continuous, that each group of life-givers came into
being owing to causes that can readily be
understood. Each group had a specific origin :
therefore the original group may likewise have
had a specific origin in the brain of a man who
first propounded the theory of a causal relationship between various objects and these vital
processes that particularly interest all men.

CHAPTER IX

THE ORIGINS OF MYTHOLOGY

ALL that is known of the growth of civilization goes to show that the fundamental arts and crafts were elaborated in the Ancient East, and then were distributed in all directions to the uttermost ends of the earth. This process of spread of civilization brought into existence communities in all stages of culture, but all deriving the whole of their cultural capital, directly or indirectly, from the original source.

The consideration of this process raises the question of the meaning of the mythological systems possessed by peoples in all outlying parts of the world. These mythologies speak continually of gods, and of the beginnings of society, and contain ideas that can be watched, more or less clearly, in process of elaboration in Egypt and other countries of the Ancient East. That these communities gained their ideas from the archaic civilization, there can be little doubt. But it remains to be seen exactly how the process worked. For, if the archaic civilization had its source at one point

on the earth's surface, and spread thence, it
might be thought that the mythological systems
of all the communities formed by the wanderers
would tend to have the same set of beliefs.   But
this is not so.   Although much similarity
can be witnessed in the beliefs of widespread
communities with regard to their beginnings,
although these similarities have caused ethnolo-
gists to formulate the doctrine of " the similarity
of the working of the human mind," in order
to explain them, yet specific differences occur
between communities that cannot be so easily
explained.

We have to inquire how the various communities of the world of early times regarded
their relationship to the world at large, and
to explain why they possessed mythologies at
all.

If we begin with the earliest signs of thought
on the relations between men and their environment, as revealed in the caves of the Upper
Palæolithic Age, we shall be impressed at once
with the fact that these early men derived
their ideas directly from experience.   They
paid attention to the cause of death, to the
nature of birth, to the means of protection.
They said to themselves, it would seem, that
the loss of blood causes death ; that the external
organ of generation gives life ; that the teeth
and claws of beasts of prey give protection,
or some such advantage, to the wearer.   Although their logic was really at fault, in that
none of these objects worn as amulets, the

shells, the red coloured substances, the teeth, were of the slightest use, yet the source of the idea is evident in every case. Therefore, when studying the use of any giver of life derived from these or other fundamental objects or substances, it must not be forgotten that all amulets have acquired their virtue ultimately from a physical phenomena that had attracted the attention of early man.

When dealing with such elementary matters as these, it might be thought that early man in all parts of the world would have come spontaneously to use identical means of deriving benefit for himself. The widespread use of red substances, of teeth, and of shells, among peoples of the lower culture, lends some support to this suggestion ; but too much stress should not be laid upon it, for there is evidence of the spread of ideas in this connection all over the world. The cowrie shell is used as an amulet in America, in Europe, and in West Africa, in places many hundreds, even thousands, of miles from the places where it exists in nature. It is therefore possible that, along with the cowrie, there has been spread the use of amulets generally. Another point that has to be remembered is that the making of the feminine figurines, characteristic of the Upper Palæolithic Age, and of the early phase of the food-producing stage of culture in the Ancient East, is confined to a relatively small area of the earth's surface, a fact of crucial importance when thinking of the history of religion. It is indeed possible, not to say probable, that the whole theory of " Givers of Life," that was worked out so minutely in later ages, was elaborated in one place ; that, for instance, the men of the Upper Palæolithic Age were the first men on the earth to use any sort of substance to protect themselves, and that the idea was spread all over the world among food-gathering peoples who never had thought of such things. The great favour shown to quartz in all parts, and the variations in the use of givers of life found in Australia, New Guinea, and Melanesia call for caution in accepting facile theories of the spontaneous development of magical practices in all parts of the world.

As culture became more complicated, after the beginning of the food-producing phase, it can readily be seen that the more complicated experience of men came to be reflected in their ideas. The Great Mother, at first a vague personality, acquired precise attributes ; but, so far as can be told, none of these attributes were the result of speculation. Barley being the shape of the cowrie, and thus acquiring its properties, the Great Mother became the Corn Mother, the personification of food. Pottery-making, metal-working, and carpentry being creative crafts, she acquired creative capacities derived from these crafts. She lived on the early civilization, and derived her qualities thence, and, from being the mother of men, she became their maker. But, here again, the dependence of early thought on experience be-

comes evident. For the Great Mother, although
she gave birth to men, and created them,
never made a place in which they could dwell.
That was left for a male being, a god. The
reason for this is obvious : irrigation from
the beginning was bound up with ruling groups,
and from the beginning also the rulers were
men, so far as can be told. The construction
of an irrigated settlement, such as Enki made
for the Sumerians at the dawn of their history,
was the work of a man, and the mother goddess
was confined to creating men. The ideas of
creation of habitable land that are found among
the Sumerians therefore bear a direct relationship to actual fact. The first act of the founders
of Sumerian civilization must have been the
reclamation of the lands, and the installation of
irrigation systems ; so, in stating that their god
made an irrigated place, the Sumerians were
recounting an historical event. The historical
nature of the story of the foundation of Sumerian
civilization is heightened by the account of
the arrival of Enki from the waters of the Persian
Gulf, he having come, according to certain
versions, in a boat. He did not come from the
sky ; he was a being of the earth. The more
these early tales are studied, the more does it
become evident that they were built up out of
early experience, and in no way are the result
of speculation. It is striking to read the recent
literature concerning the beginning of civilization in Egypt and Sumer, and to find that
places, which formerly were thought to be

fabulous, are now rapidly being identified.
It is clear that these early peoples were limited
rigorously in their thought by the conditions
in which they lived.

One of the best instances of the dependence
of men on their accumulated experience for
ideas is that of the development, in Egypt,
of the notion of a god, and of immortality.
The Egyptians, as we have seen, were led on
from one point to another, until they arrived
at the conception of the continued existence
of the spiritual part of man in another world,
and at the notion of a great being, the sun-
god, who ruled over the living, as Osiris did
over the dead.   Throughout the whole of this
process the thoughts of the Egyptian thinkers
were controlled by their circumstances, and
these men simply used ideas derived from the
conditions in which they lived.   Had it not
been for the institution of ruling classes, it is
safe to say that the idea of a god of the type
of Re, the sun-god of Egypt, would not have
emerged.   The world of gods is but the reflec-
tion of that of men, and depends entirely on
it.

In other lines of thought a like dependence
can be observed, as is evident from a study
of Elliot Smith's work on *The Evolution of the
Dragon*. The Egyptians derived their idea
of the double of man, his guardian spirit, that
was destined to become the *fravashi* of the
old Persian religion, from the homely phenom-
enon of the afterbirth ; they made the uterus,

a " giver of life " and " opener of the ways,"
into a magic wand, that would give life and
open doors ; and ideas such as these have
gone their way through the ages, and have
entirely lost their original meaning, which can
only be rescued by a careful study of the beliefs
of the country of their origin.

In seeking to express the development of
early thought by a formula, one idea must
certainly enter the minds of all who reflect on
the facts recorded in this book. No one will
fail to recognize the specific nature of early
thought. The search for some universal innate
tendency on the part of early man to elaborate
ideas about the external world, and to build
up these ideas into religious and magical
systems, must be abandoned, for such a tendency explains nothing. It seems certain that
we have to look to the inspiration of exceptional
men for all the ideas that have come into
currency. The doctrine of " the similarity of
the working of the human mind " simply
explains nothing at all ; for it ignores the
specific differences that distinguish communities
that must have lived in close contact with
one another. How can this doctrine explain
the differences between the Sumerians and the
Egyptians in their ideas about life and death ?
It is obvious to anyone that such a doctrine
breaks down completely in such a case, and
that only an historical inquiry into the cultures
of the two communities can give any explanation
of the facts ?

Of late years a new school of thought has sprung up that seeks to explain the workings of the mind on the basis of the results of the study of psycho-neuroses. If I may quote the words of the late Dr. Rivers : "There is now an extensive literature in which attempts are made to bring the symbolism of myth and ritual into relation with modern views concerning its rôle in the dream and in disease. One of the most striking conclusions to which this comparative study has led some writers is that there is a universal system of symbolization among mankind ; that among all races of mankind and in the members of every race there is a tendency to symbolize certain thoughts by means of the same symbols, or at least by symbols having a close similarity to one another " (1). He then goes on to discuss the question of re-birth ; and the rôle played by water in its ritual. The psycho-analysts claim that man universally has evolved symbols of rebirth, and that the water symbolizes the amniotic fluid. This entirely ignores the fact that the idea of rebirth is closely bound up with other notions. We have seen already that a ritual death and rebirth was supposed to procure immortality ; we have seen, moreover, that this idea was elaborated by the Egyptians in connection with their practice of mummification. There is no logical connection between rebirth and immortality. Rebirth can give a new life, but there is no reason why it should give eternal life. There-

fore, on that account, there can be no question
of universal symbolism, and the kernel of the
problem lies in the equation between two
independent ideas. The idea of rebirth is not
universal, nor is it world-wide. When it occurs
it is bound up with the idea of eternal life.
Therefore, some specific origin must be found
for the idea ; some one man must have started
the process of thought ; and until the thought
is tracked home, it cannot be understood.
Obviously vague generalizations concerning
universal tendencies are fundamentally false.
For symbols do not occur all over the world ;
they are confined to certain definite cultural
media in which they thrive, and out of which
they soon vanish.

What is the origin of the symbols used by
early man ? It seems that, in the beginning,
there were no symbols such as we recognize,
but that ideas represented concrete facts.
Men in Sumer did not speculate about the
manner in which their civilization began, they
did not elaborate ideas about gods coming
down from the sky ; they simply state baldly
that a being came up from the Persian Gulf
and founded their settlements by means of
irrigation. Man's interest, aroused by various
psychological factors, such as his fear of death,
his desire for food and for life, and so forth,
caused him to pay attention to certain phenomena, and to derive ideas from them and
from them only. He was not, in the beginning,
interested in such things as the sun, for they did

not fit into his scheme of ideas. The sun
rose and set, but that did not affect him in the
slightest : its movements were not connected
with his manner of birth or of death, or directly,
so far as he saw, with the getting of food ;
therefore it was ignored. Only when the stars
became useful as measurers of time, when the
getting of food became connected with the
observation of the heavenly bodies, did man
come to pay attention to the sun, and to use
ideas that he had acquired about moon gods,
about the Nile flood, and about creation, to
build up a new idea, that of a sun-god. The
motive of interest changed the whole situation.
When, finally, the sun-god became the father
of the king, and was thus brought into the
cycle of family cults that the Egyptian royal
family carried on, the ruling group had definite
motives for continuing the cult. Conversely,
when the Children of the Sun in any part of the
world disappeared, so did the cult of the sun-
god that they maintained, because the factors
that led the Children of the Sun to pay attention
to the sun-god were not present in the minds
of other men. Men, therefore, reason on topics
that directly interest them. Curiosity is apparently absent as a motive force causing them
indiscriminately to explore the whole external
world. There must be some directive agency,
and this is supplied by the experience of the
individual and of the community, the combination of the two determining, in general
terms, the form of thought of any given person.

For instance, it would not be expected that the idea of a god possessed by an ancient Cretan would be the same as the notion of Deity possessed by a Professor of Theology in a modern university. The two ideas would necessarily be fundamentally different. How far this difference in thought goes, to what extent the individual in early communities was conditioned by his environment, is hard to say. But it would seem that early thought was strictly limited, and possessed very little basis of speculation. Only at a late stage, say, for instance, when the Athenians started on their career of thought, were men enabled to manipulate ideas and form them into fresh combinations, as well as to allow their minds free play among phenomena. In fact, the study of science only began at a late stage of development of society, when thought had got detached from its original context, and freed itself from its early trappings.

If we turn to communities of the lower culture, and inquire into their accounts of beginnings, and into their ideas generally, it is evident at once that there is, at first sight, some difference between their systems of thought and those of the peoples of the Ancient East. Many of the ideas expressed in the tales of peoples of the lower culture are entirely speculative, if only considered in their context. Consider, for instance, the story of beginnings so common among North American Indian tribes. In the beginning there was a sky-world, populated by semi-human, semi-animal folk, while

underneath was nothing but a waste of waters.
A woman belonging to this celestial world
became with child, and, for some reason or
other, was sent away. She came down to this
earth, which had been brought up by the
otter from the depths of the sea in the form
of a small piece of mud, and when arrived on
earth, she gave birth to Twins, who created
men and civilized them. This story, as told
by Indians of North America, has nothing in
common with their experience; it certainly
has not been built up out of ideas that they
had themselves elaborated. But if it be remembered that these communities derived their
culture from Mexico, and, more remotely, from
the Ancient East, it is soon possible to understand what is at work. It is simply that these
people are explaining their mode of origin as
best they can, but that they have to use ideas
of whose original context they are ignorant.

When considering stories of this kind, two
facts must be borne in mind. Communities
of the lower culture are known to be con-
servative. Each community possesses a body
culture which is handed on from one generation
to another more or less intact, so long as no
external disturbing influence is at work. Moreover, the knowledge of myths is not the common
possession of all members of the community;
ordinary folk are only interested in matters
that directly affect themselves. For information regarding gods and their doings, reference has to be made to priests or priestesses,

as the case may be. These priests belong to an institution that can directly be ascribed to the influence of the archaic civilization, in places such as North America, Oceania and Indonesia ; no evidence exists to warrant the belief that the institution is a spontaneous growth in the midst of such communities. The ordinary people enjoy tales of their ancestors, of creation, and other more or less traditional matters, but they do not care to listen to stories of the doings of the gods. Thus it happens that a continuous process has been at work, whereby priesthoods have spread along with the archaic civilization, all of which are ultimately derived from the priesthoods of Egypt and other countries of the Ancient East.

The reason why various peoples have different tales of origins, in spite of this continuity in propagation of culture, is that these tales record, so far as is possible, the actual manner of derivation of any community from the archaic civilization, and therefore, for this reason, are as historical as the tales of the Sumerians. The more the mode of formation of fresh communities from the archaic civilization is known, the clearer become their stories of origin. In the tale just outlined, certain of the incidents are historical, while others are not. The culture-heroes, as has been seen, have an historical basis. So have the semi-human, semi-animal beings ; for they can be equated to the people of the archaic civilization, with their definite ideas as to the relationship between men and certain animals ; moreover, the animals named in this connection are the American counterparts of those that occur in connection with gods and rulers in Egypt and other countries. The notion of the primeval ocean is one that can be traced from Egypt to America, in connection with sun-gods. In Polynesia, the great hero, Maui, is said to have fished up the islands from the depths of the sea, one by one, which bears some relation to the actual history of the Polynesians, whose traditions speak of the settlement of one island after another. The incident of the kneading of earth to make a new land is evidently connected with a custom, possessed by the Polynesians, among others, of taking with them, on their travels, parcels of earth from their last home, which is to be incorporated with that of their new home. The mention only of the mother of the Twins, and the failure to say anything about the father, point to two things, to the existence of mother-right, and to the doctrine of theogamy by which these twins are universally born, these twins being, as we know definitely in certain cases, the Children of the Sun. That the mother should have come from the sky-world is another sign that she was of the archaic civilization, which was so closely connected with the sky : it is a sign, also, that her children were the Children of the Sun.

From this story, therefore, we should learn that these communities owed their civilization directly to the Children of the Sun, to beings connected with the sky-world, the place with which the Children of the Sun were actually connected, who were born by a process of theogamy. Their homeland, the sky-world, was a place where the most important beings were connected intimately with animals. The story therefore is really an historical account, mixed up with a certain amount of symbolism that the natives did not understand, of the actual mode of origin of the communities in question.

Another instance will help to make the matter plainer. The Toradja of Central Celebes have been mentioned more than once in this book. They derive their origin, as has been said, from a man and a woman who were born out of two stone images, made by a sun-god at the commands of the god of the sky and the goddess of the underworld, and animated by the wind. These beings did not receive the gift of immortality, because, when the god had gone to the sky to get the breath of life that should make them eternal, the goddess allowed the wind to blow on them and thus to animate them.

This story is quite unintelligible in all its details until the history of the Toradja is known. When their traditions with regard to the inception of their civilization is known, and when the traces of the former presence, in their lands, of men of a higher degree of civilization are recalled, much light is thrown on the account. The Children of the Sun, who formerly wandered about Central Celebes looking for gold, copper and other things, left, in places where they made settlements, carved stone images, dolmens, and other stonework. Thus the story of creation from images is unconsciously confirming the story of Lasaeo, the Sun-Lord, who civilized the branch of the Toradja in question. The incident of the animation of the images by means of breath again throws light on the ultimate provenance of the story. For, as has already been pointed out, this is the crowning incident in the ceremony of animation of portrait statues in Egypt. It is curious, moreover, how this story throws light on certain ideas of the Toradja about the nature of the soul that have become vague. It is found that the Toradja have not so clear an idea of the " life " of a man as other peoples, for instance, those of Nias. They say sometimes that it is the breath, but they are not quite certain on the matter. The creation story is definite, this shows that the idea of breath as life has been imported among the Toradja, and that it is only preserved in the lore of the priestesses.

There is one striking element in the creation story of the Toradja that still remains to be explained. Why should the Toradja claim to have missed the gift of immortality ? What has the incident of the wind animating the statues to do with reality, being, as it is, a fictitious incident ? The people who came to civilize the Toradja certainly had the belief in immortality, in connection with the practice of mummification, or in connection with certain ritual performances. We find the Toradja of the region under discussion without mummification or secret societies, or, indeed, so far as I know, any ritual of ceremonial death and rebirth. But the Toradja of the Sadang region have mummification, the making of rock-cut tombs, and many other elements of the culture of the archaic civilization, which make it probable that the group under consideration knew of this practice, and of the ideas connected with it. When, therefore, it is said that immortality was missed by their ancestors, they are stating an historical fact ; they did, somehow or other, miss it.

Stories of the way by which death came into the world are common in such places as Melanesia where the Children of the Sun must once have ruled. It is highly probable that, in all these cases, these stories recount an actual happening ; they reveal the failure of the people to take over the ritual necessary to secure immortality, the ritual which occurs in the totemic clans and in the secret societies.

A broad survey of the mythological systems of peoples of all parts of the world reveals signs of a past order, of the existence of gods, capable of wonderful feats. When the past as recorded in myths is compared with the past revealed by archæology it is found that, in proportion as knowledge accumulates on these two topics, the clearer does it become that mythologies have a place in the historical reconstruction of the outlying parts of the world. The widespread stories of the times when beings of the sky-world came to earth and mixed with men are shown to be historical by the fact that the countries where such stories are told contain material traces of the past existence of men of a phase of civilization when the rulers actually were regarded as divine beings connected with a sky-world. The conservatism of savages in preserving these accounts has provided a great mass of material of the utmost importance, the interpretation of which will serve to throw much light on the psychology of man, as on the early history of the Ancient East.

NOTES

ALTHOUGH the literature dealing with various religious and magical systems is enormous, and multitudes of facts can be obtained from such works as Sir James Frazer's *Golden Bough*, in all its ramifications, and Sir E. B. Tylor's *Primitive Culture*, yet the works dealing with the historical aspect of beliefs and practices as dealt with in this volume are few in number. The reader who wishes to follow up the historical line of thought is referred to W. H. R. Rivers, *History of Melanesian Society*, Cambridge, 1914; G. Elliot Smith, *The Migrations of Early Culture*, Manchester, 1915; *The Evolution of the Dragon*, Manchester, 1918; J. W. Jackson, *Shells as Evidence of the Migration of Early Culture*, Manchester, 1917; and the author, *Megalithic Culture of Indonesia*, Manchester, 1918; *The Children of the Sun*, London, 1923. It is on those works primarily that the argument of this book is founded, and the reader will find in them ample material evidence for statements made therein.

CHAPTER I

(1) The literature of the Palæolithic Age is considerable. The reader will find material ready to hand in such works as M. Burkitt, *Prehistory*, Cambridge, 1922; J. Déchelette, *Manuel d'archéologie celtique et gauloise*, Paris, 1908; H. F. Osborn, *Men of the Old Stone Age*, London, 1921; W. J. Sollas, *Ancient Hunters and their Modern Representatives*, 2nd edition, London, 1915.

(2) J. W. Jackson, *Shells as Evidence of the Migration of Early Culture*, Manchester, 1917, pp. 135-7. It is full

of information directly related to the thesis of this book.

(3) G. Elliot Smith, *The Evolution of the Dragon*, Manchester, 1918. A book of fundamental importance for the study of the origins of religion and magic. Most of the argument of the early chapters of this book is taken from it, with modifications. The reader will find there ample references for the facts adduced.

(4) Elliot Smith, op. cit., p. 150.

(5) *Ibid.*, p. 150–1.

(6) *Ibid.*, p. 145.

(7) J. W. Jackson, loc. cit.

(8) Elliot Smith, op. cit., pp. 165 *et seq.*

(9) Déchelette, op. cit., III, pp. 1547 *et seq.*

(10) Elliot Smith, op. cit., pp. 221 *et seq.*

(11) *Ibid.*, p. 153.

(12) *Ibid.*, p. 151. The third chapter of this book, entitled The Birth of Aphrodite, is a mine of information about the Great Mother. The reader will find there full references for the facts quoted in the following pages. See also D. Mackenzie, *Myths of Crete aud pre-Hellenic Europe*, for a good account of the Great Mother.

(13) A. J. Evans, *The Palace of Minos*, Chapter II ; also Salomon Reinach, *Les Déesses Nues dans l'Art Oriental et dans l'Art Grec.*, Rev. Archeol., Vol. 26, 1895 ; also the same in l'Anthropologie, Vol. 5.

(14) Donald A. Mackenzie, *Ancient Man in Britain*, Edinburgh, 1923. Chapter XII.

(15) W. G. Aston, *Shinto : The Way of the Gods*, London, 1905.

CHAPTER II

(1) The credit of having realized the significance of the Nile Flood cycle belongs to Professor T. Cherry. See his paper, *The Discovery of Agriculture*, Australasian Association for the Advancement of Science, 1921.

(2) L. W. King, *A History of Sumer and Akkad*, London, 1910. S. Langdon, *Tammuz and Ishtar*, Oxford, 1914 ; *Le poème sumérien du paradis, du déluge et de la chute*

de l'homme, Paris, 1919. A. Poebel, *Historical Texts,* University of Pennsylvania. Publications of the Babylonian Section, Vol. 4, No. 1, 1914.

(3) Elliot Smith, op. cit., p. 29.

(4) Perry, *The Children of the Sun,* London, 1923, pp. 440–2.

(5) J. H. Breasted, *Development of Religion and Thought in Ancient Egypt,* London, 1912 ; Elliot Smith, op. cit., pp. 24 *et seq.,* pp. 29 *et seq.*

(6) Elliot Smith, op. cit., p. 32.

(7) Perry, op. cit., pp. 439–42.

(8) See Elliot Smith, op. cit., p. 109, for a discussion of this story. A translation of the story is given in Budge's *Legends of the Gods,* London, 1912.

(9) Breasted, *Ancient Records of Egypt,* London, 1907. II, §§ 188 *et seq.*

(10) A detailed account will be found in Perry, op. cit., Chapter XXVI.

CHAPTER III

(1) Elliot Smith, *The Migrations of Early Culture,* Manchester, 1915, gives a detailed account of the development of Egyptian funerary customs, pp. 32 *et seq.*

(2) Langdon, *Le poème sumérien du paradis, du déluge et de la chute de l'homme,* pp. 91–2.

(3) Elliot Smith, *The Evolution of the Dragon,* pp. 15 *et seq.* ; *Migrations,* pp. 37 *et seq.*

(4) Breasted, *Development of Religion and Thought,* pp. 56, 61.

(5) A. M. Blackman, *The Significance of Incense and Libations in Funerary and Temple Ritual,* Zeitschrift für Aegyptische Sprache, p. 50, 1912.

(6) A good account of the ritual of mummification is given by (Sir) E. A. W. Budge, *The Mummy,* Cambridge, 1893.

(7) Elliot Smith, *Migrations,* p. 42.

(8) Breasted, *A History of Egypt,* London, 1919, pp. 51, 69.

(9) Breasted, *Development of Religion and Thought,* p. 143.

CHAPTER IV

This chapter is based on material collected in the following of my publications, *The Isles of the Blest*, Folk-
Lore, 1921 ; *The Megalithic Culture of Indonesia*, Manchester, 1918 ; *War and Civilization*, Manchester, 1918 ;
The Children of the Sun ; *An Interpretation of Old Testa-
ment Tradition*, Journal of the Manchester Egyptian and
Oriental Society (1921–2), 1923. See also *The Growth
of Civilization* for a fuller treatment of some aspects of the
spread of early culture.

(1) Ezekiel xxviii. 11 *et seq.* makes it clear that Eden
was regarded as an actual place on the earth that could be
inhabited by men.

(2) T. E. Peet, *Rough Stone Monuments*, London, 1912,
gives a fairly good account of the distribution of megalithic monuments.   He, however, does not mention America, both parts of which continent contain typical examples.

(3) Elliot Smith, *The Origin of the Dolmen*, Rep. Brit.
Ass. 1913, Man., 1913 ; *The Evolution of the Rock-Cut
Tomb and the Dolmen*, Essays and Studies presented to
William Ridgeway, Cambridge, 1913. O. G. S. Crawford
(Ordnance Survey, Professional Papers, New Series, No.
6, 1922) has acknowledged the truth of Elliot Smith's
contention in respect of the Long Barrows of England, the
structure of which resembles that of an Egyptian mastaba.
Karge (*Rephaim* : die vorgeschichtliche Kultur Palästinas
und Phöniziens, 8vo, Paderborn, 1917) has also independently recognized the similarity between Egyptian pyramid
and mastaba tombs and dolmens, but he has not realized
the part played by degradation in the process of spread of
culture.

(4) F. H. Nichols, *Through Hidden Shensi*, London, 1902.
pp. 243 *et seq.*

(5) Langdon, *Le poème sumérien.*

(6) For an interesting discussion of this problem see
papers by Dr. S. Langdon and Dr. W. F. Albright in Vols.
6 and 7 of the *Journal of Egyptian Archæology*, 1920, 1921.

CHAPTER V

The reader will find detailed discussions of the evidence adduced in this and the following chapters in *The Megalithic Culture of Indonesia*, and *The Children of the Sun*, to which books he is referred.

(1) R. N. Hall and W. G. Neal, *The Ancient Ruins of Rhodesia*, London, 1904.

CHAPTER VI

(1) Aston, *Shinto* ; M. Revon, *Le Shinntoisme*, Paris, 1907.

CHAPTER VII

(1) See *Mysteries* in Hastings' *Encyclopœdia of Religion and Ethics* ; also J. G. Frazer, *Adonis, Attis, Osiris*, London, 1906.

(2) F. Cumont, *The Mysteries of Mithra*, London, 1903 ; *Textes et monuments figurés relatifs aux mystères de Mithra*, Brussels, 1896, 1899.

(3) W. J. Hoffman, *The Mide'wiwin or Grand Medicine Society of the Ojibwa*, 7th Annual Report of the Bureau of Ethnology, Washington, 1885–6.

(4) E. R. Emerson, *The Book of the Dead and Rain Ceremonials*, American Anthropologist, 7, 1894.

CHAPTER VIII

(1) C. Blinkenberg, *The Thunderweapon in Religion and Folk-lore*, Easton, 1916.

CHAPTER IX

(1) *Folk-Lore*, 1922, p. 18.

APPENDIX

SINCE this book was set up in type, I have found it possible to explain the change of name that occurs in connection with Mystery Religions, secret societies and initiation ceremonies in all parts of the world.

The novice who has died and been reborn is considered to be a new individual. Why should this be ? He is really the same person. The answer is provided by a consideration of the practice of mummification in Egypt, out of which has arisen the notion that ritual, death and rebirth confer immortality. One important feature of the practice of mummification was the belief that the person mummified became some one else. It was thought that the king, who during life was Horus, became Osiris after his death ; that is to say, he changed his name and identity. This was the fiction in every case of mummification : whether the person mummified was the king or not, he was believed to have become Osiris after the process. It is thus easy to see how the idea could have arisen that every one who had undergone the process of ritual death and rebirth should have to change his name and become some one else. For the fiction of change of personality was taken over together with the other ideas in connection with mummification. The novice secured immortality by virtue of the fact that he was some one else.

INDEX